Samaritan Journey

This is a book for our times! In the midst of a pandemic and in anticipation of the Catholic community's Plenary 2021, *Samaritan Journey* captures the spirit of contemporary Australians – a spirit of hope in anxiety, a spirit of truth in uncertainty, a spirit of love in complexity. The title implies a challenge; it is never easy to choose the 'road less travelled', but Margaret Ghosn ensures that there will be companionship on the way. Her book is, indeed, an invaluable guide. It explores a highly controversial human story in the New Testament – that of the Good Samaritan. She takes us on a journey that invites personal reflection, offers insightful scriptural commentary, provides a depth of wisdom, and confronts our human foibles. Going off the beaten track is not for the faint-hearted. This book takes us to the raw edge of life in this new decade. I would say that it is a book not just to be read but rather, one to be truly listened to. Take the journey... and take your time!

Sr Jill Shirvington OP

Dominican Sisters of Eastern Australia and the Solomon Islands

In *Samaritan Journey - Compassion, subversion and discipleship*, the author takes you on a comprehensive and insightful journey into the parable of the Good Samaritan. On this journey, you will be presented with an in-depth explanation of how a simple story has influenced the lives of millions of people throughout the millennia and helped guide and shape Western political, humanitarian, legal, artistic and educational traditions from the United Nations *Declaration of Human Rights* to the local soup kitchen.

Margaret Ghosn's book clearly demonstrates why the parable is as counter cultural today as it was when it was first spoken because it challenges us to leave our comfort zones, throw away our prejudices and focus on the needs of the suffering wherever they may be. *Samaritan Journey - Compassion, subversion and discipleship* is both deeply spiritual and eminently practical as it calls us to follow the Great Commandment of Christ to love God and others. After reading, it you will appreciate why the Good Samaritan is one of Jesus' greatest of parables.

Maronite Deacon Ron Hassarati
Author *The One thing God cannot do* and *Found by God*.

This thought-provoking book, *Samaritan journey* is worthy of personal reflection or group discussion. Margaret Ghosn takes us on another's road. She skilfully interweaves Jesus' way of being, biblical texts, insights of highly admired people and contemporary events within each verse of this famous parable.

The Good Samaritan has inspired and continues to inspire countless acts of compassion for and companioning of others.

The author is not critical of the characters but recognises in each how and why people might react in similar circumstances. The challenge for the reader's life is practical, everyday application of loving the other as oneself and our responsibility to our common home in its ecological crisis.

Diann Hynes
School Consultant, Diocese of Broken Bay.

COMPASSION
SUBVERSION AND
DISCIPLESHIP

SAMARITAN JOURNEY

MARGARET GHOSN

COVENTRY
PRESS

Published in Australia by
Coventry Press
33 Scoresby Road
Bayswater Vic. 3153
Australia

ISBN 9780648861218

Copyright © Margaret Ghosn 2020

All rights reserved. Other than for the purposes and subject to the conditions prescribed under the *Copyright Act*, no part of this publication may be reproduced, stored in a retrieval system, or transmitted in any form or by any means, electronic, mechanical, photocopying, recording or otherwise, without the prior permission of the publisher.

Scripture quotations are from the *New Revised Standard Version Bible*, copyright 1989, Division of Christian Education of the National Council of the Churches of Christ in the United States of America. Used by permission. All rights reserved.

Cataloguing-in-Publication entry is available from the National Library of Australia http://catalogue.nla.gov.au/.

Cover design by Ian James - www.jgd.com.au
Text design by Megan Low (Film Shot Graphics FSG)
Set in PT Serif

Printed in Australia

Contents

Foreword 9

Introduction
A journey with the parable of the Good Samaritan 13

Chapter 1
Intentions for the journey 21

Chapter 2
Purpose of the journey 37

Chapter 3
Companions on the journey 52

Chapter 4
The journey begins with trouble on the horizon. 64

Chapter 5
The passersby 92

Chapter 6
Stopping on the journey 127

Chapter 7
Getting off the beaten track 149

Chapter 8
Back on the road again 165

Chapter 9
    The cost of being on the road *175*

Chapter 10
    The road ahead *190*

Bibliography. *203*

Foreword

I was intrigued to hear it said that if the Gospel of Luke was performed as musical theatre, the accompanying melodies would sound hauntingly familiar because they would reprise the entire Gospel. We would hear the joyful chorales that accompanied healings and the whimsical jingles created each time Jesus outsmarted leaders and lawyers. With this thought in mind I read with interest Sister Margaret's book, *Samaritan Journey: Compassion, subversion and discipleship*.

The Bible has begun to occupy an important place in the life of God's people. Pope Francis reminds us that it is 'the book of the Lord's people, and moves all who listen to it, to move from dispersion towards unity for the word of God unites believers and makes them one people'. He assures us that the Bible is the means by which we develop a closer relationship with Jesus who speaks to everyone with his Word and we, with open hearts and minds, allow this Jesus to enter our lives and remain ever with us.

With depth of scholarship and broad reading, Sister Margaret's ten chapters inject new life into, and perhaps surface forgotten challenges, in a familiar story that leaves it ringing in our ears, if not on our lips. The author has the ability to remind us how Christ is present, speaking to us, and wishes to be heard.[1]

Each chapter begins with words from the parable, words explored in the context of life experience, with accompanying questions and challenges, offering material for personal reflection, retreats, faith group conversations, RCIA seekers who desire a deeper relationship with the Risen Christ.

As a good teacher, and herself attuned to the power of the Word, Margaret engages us with the story in a way that reminds us how the Bible is not just the heritage of some, much less a collection of books for the benefit of a privileged few; rather, it belongs to all who hear its message and recognise themselves in its words. Her work invites into the story whereby we become the story, we are the Good Samaritan!

I began with the comment about the Gospel of Luke as a musical. If it were a musical, we would keep learning its songs, comprehending their meaning in ever-deeper ways and learning to appreciate the story's endless capacity for the harmonies that can only come from a great diversity of voices.

But the point is not to be a choir, but to perform the Gospel, off stage, on the road, wherever we are. This is where Margaret's insight and practical pathways into

---

1   *Verbum Domini* #56

the familiar story has led me and where I hope all who read Sister Margaret's book will be led, and see that embracing a 'Samaritan Journey', the Gospel stories truly are hauntingly familiar because they reprise the whole Gospel.

Rev. Dr John Frauenfelder
Head of Theology/Deputy Principal
BBI - The Australian Institute of Theological Education

Introduction

A journey with the parable of the Good Samaritan

Pope Francis understands the relevance of the Scriptures for our lives today, as he clearly wrote in his Apostolic letter *Aperuit Illis*: 'The relationship between the Risen Lord, the community of believers and sacred Scripture is essential to our identity as Christians… The Bible is the book of the Lord's people'.[2] Indeed, the Bible is a book that can speak so much to the individual and to the community. One such example is that of the parable of the Good Samaritan in the Gospel of Luke, Chapter 10, verses 25 to 37. Let us take look at this passage:

---

2   Pope Francis' Apostolic letter, *Aperuit Illis*, Instituting the Sunday of the Word of God, 30 September 2019, paragraphs 1 and 4.

http://www.vatican.va/content/francesco/en/motu_proprio/documents/papa-francesco-motu-proprio-20190930_aperuit-illis.html

Just then a lawyer stood up to test Jesus. 'Teacher', he said, 'what must I do to inherit eternal life?' He said to him, 'What is written in the law? What do you read there?' He answered, 'You shall love the Lord your God with all your heart, and with all your soul, and with all your strength, and with all your mind; and your neighbour as yourself'. And he said to him, 'You have given the right answer; do this, and you will live'.

But wanting to justify himself, he asked Jesus, 'And who is my neighbour?' Jesus replied, 'A man was going down from Jerusalem to Jericho, and fell into the hands of robbers, who stripped him, beat him, and went away, leaving him half dead. Now by chance a priest was going down that road; and when he saw him, he passed by on the other side. So likewise a Levite, when he came to the place and saw him, passed by on the other side. But a Samaritan while travelling came near him; and when he saw him, he was moved with pity. He went to him and bandaged his wounds, having poured oil and wine on them. Then he put him on his own animal, brought him to an inn, and took care of him. The next day he took out two denarii, gave them to the innkeeper, and said, "Take care of him; and when I come back, I will repay you whatever more you spend". Which of these three, do you think, was a neighbour to the man who fell into the hands of the robbers?' He said, 'The one who showed him mercy'. Jesus said to him, 'Go and do likewise'.

The parable of the Good Samaritan is one such story that transcends time, speaking to all generations, across centuries. It is one of the more popular and well known parables of Jesus and is a wonderful piece of storytelling that hits home with a punch. It is about social justice, boundary dismantling, willing service, community building, loving God, loving neighbour and eternal life. It is, in short, a timeless classic.

The parable of the Good Samaritan is located in the Gospel of Luke. Whatever opinion one holds in regards to the Bible and the messages there, we should not be too ready to dismiss it as being irrelevant or preachy. If we honour what has been handed down over the centuries, then no matter who we are, we will recognise that there is truth and value in sacred texts. In fact, the Good Samaritan resulted in the Church building numerous hospices, hospitals and charities, including Samaritan's Purse, a non-profit, Christian organisation providing emergency relief and development assistance to suffering people around the world, with the aim of demonstrating God's love.[3]

The parable of the Good Samaritan has also influenced legislations across nations. One such example is the NSW *Civil Liability Act*, that states in Part 8:56 that a *good samaritan* is a person who, in good faith and without expectation of payment or other reward, comes to the assistance of a person who is apparently injured or at risk of being injured.[4]

Although many people may choose – for whatever reason – not to be the Good Samaritan to an injured stranger, the ideal of helping another remains highly valued.

By asking the everyday person what this parable is trying to teach us, it is evident that values such as help, love, mercy and equality are vital. Here are some insights that people of different walks of life have offered:

> To be good to all people no matter who they are. To feel with people. Jesus is teaching us to love even our enemies but the problem is how can you love someone who hurts you? (Male, 79 years of age)

---

3   Samaritan's Purse. International relief Australia and New Zealand. https://www.samaritanspurse.org.au/who-we-are/about-samaritans-purse/

4   NSW, the Civil Liability Act https://www.legislation.nsw.gov.au/#/view/act/2002/22/part8

The one who helps is the one who is teaching us love. To love one another and help each other. (Female, 73 years of age)

Mercy has no boundaries or nationality or personality. Mercy has no limits. (Female, 57 years of age)

Some people are comfortable in their own skin and are not fussed about others. People should help others because they want too, not because they're obliged to. (Male, 45 years of age)

Compassion has no boundaries. You shouldn't judge people based on their religion. Enemies can be your neighbours. (Female, 27 years of age)

To always help someone in need even if they are different to you. To show mercy to others even if we do not know them. –Female 13 years of age

So why should we listen to Jesus' parable? It is, as the comments suggest, because truth is revealed to us, if we care to listen.

Eternal truths are not irrelevant. They may not be evident in the daily actions of our busy lives, but they pulsate in our veins and when we do hear them, they resonate deeply in us and awaken a new dimension to our being. They draw us into an awakening to so much more than the superfluous nature we all too often inhabit.

The parable of the Good Samaritan expresses in its own unique way, what we all deeply desire to attain. A desire to be open and generous, caring and welcoming, warm and healing, in a world that holds so much contradiction, hurt and deception. The desire to offer great hope and to welcome with healing love is an important message of the parable. A contemporary way of putting this was captured on a Facebook post by an unknown author:

> As the world fights to figure everything out,
> I'll be holding doors for strangers,
> Letting people cut in front of me in traffic,
> Saying good morning,
> Keeping babies entertained in grocery lines,
> Stopping to talk to someone who is lonely,
> Being patient with sales clerks,
> Smiling at a passerby.
> WHY?

Because I will not stand idly by and
Live in a world where love is invisible.
Join me in showing kindness,
Understanding, and judging less.
Be kind to a stranger,
Give grace to friends who are having a bad day,
Be forgiving of yourself – today and everyday.

Who knows, but perhaps this writer was reflecting on the Good Samaritan, as they composed this, since it captures the essence of the parable.

Much can be said about the parable, and much can be written or rephrased. Verse after verse speaks volumes and if we examine the parable more closely, more insights and more demands face us. Becoming a Samaritan is choosing to be, or even finding ourselves to be:

- The odd one out
- The one looked upon with suspicion
- The disliked one
- The vulnerable one
- The one targeted

To be a 'good' Samaritan is to:

- Go against stereotypes
- Do the unexpected

- Lead the way
- Reveal one's humanitarian nature
- Do what others refuse to do
- Buck the trend

The journey to become a Good Samaritan is a journey of opposition, unexpected twists and turns. It is a journey to becoming what we thought or had presumed we could not be or do. It will take us into 'danger' territory where we will have to show courage to choose the path to take, despite road blockages from people who want to make others conform to a false pattern or image. It is to listen to the voice of pain calling out to us on the journey. It is to see the obstacles on the road as opportunities to change and become who we are meant to be. It is to be bold enough to take the narrow road and not a detour that avoids any challenges.

So let us travel on the road and be open to the truths that speak to us on the journey. Let us learn what it means to be a neighbour, to recognise who is our neighbor, and to be challenged by the figure of the Good Samaritan. Let us venture off the beaten track into new territory.

Chapter 1

Intentions for the journey

> *Just then a lawyer stood up to test Jesus. 'Teacher,' he said, 'what must I do to inherit eternal life?' He said to him, 'What is written in the law? What do you read there?'*
>
> Luke 10:25-26

Just then a lawyer stood up to test Jesus...

The setting and context of the parable of the Good Samaritan is similar to other 'controversy' stories in the Gospels. A controversy story has a regular sequence of elements:

1) an action by Jesus or his disciples

2) stimulates a challenge from opponents which leads to

3) a pronouncement by Jesus that is a well formed statement of a more general application. Some examples are seen below:

And as he sat at dinner in Levi's house, many tax-collectors and sinners were also sitting with Jesus and his disciples – for there were many who followed him. When the scribes of the Pharisees saw that he was eating with sinners and tax-collectors, they said to his disciples, 'Why does he eat with tax-collectors and sinners?' When Jesus heard this, he said to them, 'Those who are well have no need of a physician, but those who are sick; I have come to call not the righteous but sinners'.
Now John's disciples and the Pharisees were fasting; and people came and said to him, 'Why do John's disciples and the disciples of the Pharisees fast, but your disciples do not fast?' Jesus said to them, 'The wedding-guests cannot fast while the bridegroom is with them, can they? As long as they have the bridegroom with them, they cannot fast. The days will come when the bridegroom is taken away from them, and then they will fast on that day.

Mark 2:15-20

Some Pharisees came, and to test him they asked, 'Is it lawful for a man to divorce his wife?' He answered them, 'What did Moses command you?' They said, 'Moses allowed a man to write a certificate of dismissal and to divorce her'. But Jesus said to them, 'Because of your hardness of heart he wrote this commandment for you. But from the beginning of creation, "God made them male and female". "For this reason a man shall leave his father and mother and be joined to his wife, and the two shall become one flesh." So they are no longer two, but one flesh. Therefore what God has joined together, let no one separate.'

Mark 10:2-9

In the parable of the Good Samaritan, we read in the passage prior to the parable, of Jesus sending out seventy-two disciples (other Gospels mention seventy) on mission, and follows their success with praising God, 'At that same hour Jesus rejoiced in the Holy Spirit and said, "I thank you, Father, Lord of heaven and earth, because you have hidden these things from the wise and the intelligent and have revealed them to infants; yes, Father, for such was your gracious will"' (Luke 10:21). What follows is the discussion between the lawyer and Jesus and then we are introduced to the parable of the Good Samaritan. The lawyer, one of 'the wise and intelligent' that Jesus mentioned earlier, poses a question, 'What must I do to inherit eternal life?' Jesus then makes a pronouncement about neighbour, not what the lawyer expected!

The parable commences with a challenge to Jesus by a lawyer. Many times, when rabbis 'tested,' it was not done with hostile intentions. The rabbinic style of public discussion was to pose difficult questions with the expectation of debate, explains Lois Tverberg. Questions like whether divorce was permissible, or what was the greatest commandment, were important discussions permeating the rabbinic community of Jesus' time.[5]

The parable of the Good Samaritan (Luke 10:25–37) is framed within Jesus' conversation with a lawyer, an expert in the Jewish law. The parable provides a pedagogical context of question-answer in which to understand the parable.

When the lawyer questions Jesus, he wants to know who Jesus really is. Jesus has spent his days among the people teaching, preaching and witnessing. He performs miracles, shows compassion, heals, forgives and loves. Yet there remain those who question.

Jesus is aware of the lawyer's purpose for questioning and shortly after the parable of the Good Samaritan, Jesus condemns lawyers by stating in Luke 11:46, 'Woe also to you lawyers! For you load people with burdens hard to bear, and you yourselves do not lift a finger to ease them'. It was a scathing attack on lawyers who did not put their knowledge to good use, but rather used it to judge and condemn others unfairly.

What was the lawyer's intention? What are our

---

5   Lois Tverberg, Jesus' *Surprising Answer* 5 June 2019. https://engediresourcecenter.com/2019/06/05/jesus-surprising-answer/

intentions? Our attitude to God and to one another determines how we see. If we approach with an open mind and heart, willing to witness to the truth, then we will be rewarded with insight. If we approach, already filled with doubts, questions and negativity, we may struggle to see the truth before our very eyes.

Yet taking another angle to the story, we can view the lawyer's question as a necessary step each of us should boldly take. Can we challenge the *status quo*? Do we dare to step up and speak out? Often our willingness to speak up, come forward, question or challenge, can appear as too radical, or too threatening. Perhaps the lawyer's original question and challenge is a great example to us, of speaking our minds and being willing to question and provoke. Maybe we have taken Christianity and used it to solace the crowds, blockade any upsurges and insist on conformity. We are encouraged to be nice, put our heads down, walk on, and do the 'right thing'. We are not meant to disturb the peace. Yet the lawyer wants to disrupt and disturb, and Jesus in return is willing to court danger.

Like the lawyer, perhaps there are times when we do ask the questions that are on our mind, but we soon discover that with God, we may be led to answers which we probably do not always want to hear. In approaching God with our questions and our challenges, God leads us off the beaten track, walking us away from our self-centredness and egotistical desires, onto a road far removed from our little world. The lawyer had asked a question, hoping for a particular response. Instead, he was led to another way of thinking. So are we prepared not only to ask the question, but – more importantly – are we prepared to hear the truth? As Jesus says in Luke 11:9, 'So I say to you, ask, and it will be given to you; search, and you will find; knock, and the door will be opened for you'. But what is given and what is found and what is opened to you may come as a surprise!

What must I do to inherit eternal life?

The same question the lawyer poses to Jesus, 'What must I do to inherit eternal life?' is also later put to Jesus by a certain ruler:

> A certain ruler asked him, 'Good Teacher, what must I do to inherit eternal life?' Jesus said to him, 'Why do you call me good? No one is good but God alone. You know the commandments: "You shall not commit adultery; You shall not murder; You shall not steal; You shall not bear false witness; Honour your father and mother."' He replied, 'I have kept all these since my youth'. When Jesus heard this, he said to him, 'There is still one thing lacking. Sell all that you own and distribute the money to the poor, and you will have treasure in heaven; then come, follow me'. But when he heard this, he

became sad; for he was very rich. Jesus looked at him and said, 'How hard it is for those who have wealth to enter the kingdom of God! Indeed, it is easier for a camel to go through the eye of a needle than for someone who is rich to enter the kingdom of God'.

Luke 18:18-25

In both cases, we have the word 'good'. In Luke 18:18, Jesus is given the title, 'Good Teacher' and in our parable, the Samaritan is generally referred to as the 'Good Samaritan'. Yet Jesus has a word to say in regards to 'good'. He warns the ruler, 'Why do you call me good?' (Luke 18:19). We might also ask, why do we call the Samaritan good? We are not called to be good. We are called to do what is right and that may mean boundary pushing, barrier dismantling, going against the *status quo*. It may be that we are asked to be bold and radical.

In both the parable of the Good Samaritan and the story of the certain ruler, the same pattern of events occurs. The lawyer and ruler begin with a question and then further probing, followed by the same response from Jesus. To the ruler's question, 'Good Teacher, what must I do to inherit eternal life?' (18:18), the response – according to Jesus – is to follow the commandments of the Torah. And again the certain ruler wants to probe further. So Jesus insists that the money be put to the service of the poor. It proves to be a difficult call for the ruler.

Both the lawyer and the certain ruler want to go deeper, not satisfied at the level they are at. They are a reflection of each of us, with the constant desire to question, to go deeper than the surface of our lives, and not just remain in the shallow end. As the lawyer and the ruler are drawn to Jesus, he also draws us to a deeper level of thinking. Questioning and doubting are doors to new insights, but we must let go of our current patterns and be challenged by the very things we distance ourselves from. When pushed further by Jesus, do we baulk at what is demanded of us?

So the question is posed, 'What must I do to inherit eternal life?' James writes in his Letter, 'So faith by itself, if it has no works, is dead' (James 2:17). We are people of faith but also people of action. The parable of the Good Samaritan says no less. It is to show your faith through your actions.

Life is not to be calculated, lived in fear; it is not about getting into the good books, earning points; nor is it to be focused only on our salvation. Eternal life is not inherited. It is not merited. The motivation to live this life should not be based on dying for the next life. Love this life first and the rest of life is yours. As Jesus said, 'I came that they may have life, and have it abundantly' (John 10:10). To have life abundantly is to love fully, unconditionally, without counting the cost.

When we begin to count the cost, narrow our vision, limit our efforts, focus solely on ourselves, ignore the current reality for a spiritual future, we are not living the fullness of life we have the capacity for, and so we stunt our growth. The parable of the Good Samaritan and the story of the certain ruler both challenge us to do all we can for one another in this present life, here and now.

He said to him...

In the Gospels, Jesus is asked a total of 183 questions, with most repeated at least once more in other synoptic Gospels. Yet, Jesus never answers questions directly but elicits a response from the other. He arouses their curiosity and invites the other to question deeper. This is what is termed a Socratic technique. Jesus does not give answers but leads each of us to our liminal space, the threshold of where we are, and it is here we are called to be.

Jesus responds to the lawyer's two questions not with answers but with further questions, 'What is written in the law? What do you read there?' (10:26) and 'Which of these three, do you think, was a neighbour to the man who fell into the hands of the robbers?' (10:36). Jesus only gives answers in response to the answers the lawyer gives (10:28, 37).

When Jesus responds to questions with another question – as he often does in the Gospel accounts – he is inviting us to participate actively in exploring answers to our questions. Another such example – also in Luke's Gospel – is as follows:

> Others, to test him, kept demanding from him a sign from heaven. But he knew what they were thinking and said to them, 'Every kingdom divided against itself becomes a desert, and house falls on house. If Satan also is divided against himself, how will his kingdom stand? – for you say that I cast out the demons by Beelzebul. Now if I cast out the demons by Beelzebul, by whom do your exorcists cast them out? Therefore they will be your judges.
>
> Luke 11:16-19

Yet, there are also instances when Jesus questions in order to challenge and coax us out of narrow-minded views:

> Just then, in front of him, there was a man who had dropsy. And Jesus asked the lawyers and Pharisees, 'Is it lawful to cure people on the sabbath, or not?' But they were silent. So Jesus took him and healed him, and sent him away.
>
> Luke 14:2-4

There are also times when Jesus responds to questions in ways his challengers would never have anticipated:

> Once Jesus was asked by the Pharisees when the kingdom of God was coming, and he answered, 'The kingdom of God is not coming with things that can be observed; nor will they say, "Look, here it is!" or "There it is!" For, in fact, the kingdom of God is among you.'
>
> Luke 17:20-21

> So they watched him and sent spies who pretended to be honest, in order to trap him by what he said, so as to hand him over to the jurisdiction and authority of the governor. So they asked him, 'Teacher, we know that you are right in what you say and teach, and you show deference to no one, but teach the way of God in accordance with truth. Is it lawful for us to pay taxes to the emperor, or not?' But he perceived their craftiness and said to them, 'Show me a denarius. Whose head and whose title does it bear?' They said, 'The emperor's.' He said to them, 'Then give to the emperor the things that are the emperor's, and to God the things that are God's'. And they were not able in the presence of the people to trap him by what he said; and being amazed by his answer, they became silent.
>
> Luke 20:20-26

> One day, as he was teaching the people in the temple and telling the good news, the chief priests and the scribes came with the elders and said to him, 'Tell us, by what authority are you doing these things? Who is it who gave you this authority?' He answered them, 'I will also ask you a question, and you tell me: Did the baptism of John come from heaven, or was it of human origin?'
>
> Luke 20:1-4

And then there are times where Jesus does not respond at all to questions posed to him:

> When Herod saw Jesus, he was very glad, for he had been wanting to see him for a long time, because he had heard about him and was hoping to see him perform some sign. He questioned him at some length, but Jesus gave him no answer.
>
> Luke 23:8-9

In not responding, Jesus knew he could not change the mind of those who were not prepared to listen. As he repeatedly says, 'looking they may not perceive, and listening they may not understand' (Luke 8:10). Perhaps we need to think twice before we pose a question and ask what is our intention in doing so.

More so, perhaps we should think twice before we respond to a question!

'What is written in the law? What do you read there?'

'What is written in the Law?' Jesus questions the lawyer who would have been all too familiar with the law. The problem was not lack of knowledge of the law, but its interpretation. Yet, before even debating the law, there is the assumption one can read the law.

To read is to be literate, something many of us take for granted. We barely cast a thought to those who are illiterate or forbidden access to particular written material. Seventeen percent of the world's population is illiterate. There has been an increase in literacy over the decades which is a move in the right direction; yet even among literate people, millions are denied access to current information about events happening in the world. And in more recent times, 'fake news' has become prominent globally, calling into question the truth of what we hear and read. In fact, what can we believe? To make things even more complicated, we see student literacy falling annually. What will this mean for the future, when people have a lower grasp of literacy and are face to face with fake news? How will truth be discerned?

Still on the topic of literacy: what we read is subjective. What we read and understand and take on board, matters and influences our actions; and is in turn influenced by our experiences. The written law is one thing but our reading of it is another. We must ask: what influences our perception and understanding of the law, or of anything, for that matter.

So the lawyer asks, 'What is written in the law?' How do we decide on what is law and what is not? More often than not, legislation is passed not to encourage particular practices but to decriminalise them. One such example is legislation for full term abortion. Many voiced concerns over its implementation in the Australian State of NSW, but ultimately it is the Government Body that votes and each party has its own political agenda. So if the Bill is passed, it is not so much about whether this law is now deemed just, but whether it serves the interest of the people (or the party). Curiously enough, the parable equates eternal life with the law. Perhaps this is a nudge at any law that does not promote life!

So what is written in the law? The lawyer responds to Jesus by quoting the law of loving God with your whole heart, but he could have quoted many other laws – abiding by rituals, offering burnt sacrifices, avoiding the impure, or the ten commandments (Exodus 20:1-17; Deuteronomy 5:6-21). These were laws that all Jews were expected to follow and know.

Elsewhere in Luke's Gospel, the laws for inheriting eternal life involve:

Blessed are you who are poor, for yours is the kingdom of God. (Luke 6:20)

But love your enemies, do good, and lend, expecting nothing in return. Your reward will be great, and you will be children of the Most High. (Luke 6:35)

Then he said to them all, 'If any want to become my followers, let them deny themselves and take up their cross daily and follow me. For those who want to save their life will lose it, and those who lose their life for my sake will save it. (Luke 9:23-24)

Jesus said to him, 'No one who puts a hand to the plough and looks back is fit for the kingdom of God'. (Luke 9:62)

Someone asked him, 'Lord, will only a few be saved?' He said to them, 'Strive to enter through the narrow door; for many, I tell you, will try to enter and will not be able'. (Luke 13:23-24)

Truly I tell you, whoever does not receive the kingdom of God as a little child will never enter it. (Luke 18:17)

And he said to them, 'Truly I tell you, there is no one who has left house or wife or brothers or

> parents or children, for the sake of the kingdom of God, who will not get back very much more in this age, and in the age to come eternal life'. (Luke 18:29-30)

Yet in Luke's Gospel, Jesus is not so much focused on the law for eternal life but on the present. In fact. Jesus shows minimal interest in teaching about laws on eternal life. His focus is on our behaviour at this moment, here and now.

> Once Jesus was asked by the Pharisees when the kingdom of God was coming, and he answered, 'The kingdom of God is not coming with things that can be observed; nor will they say, "Look, here it is!" or "There it is!" For, in fact, the kingdom of God is among you'. (Luke 17:20-21)

So what becomes law for us? Do we seek laws that lead us to live this life fully? Are we prepared and willing to follow the law of love?

Chapter 2

Purpose of the journey

> *He answered, 'You shall love the Lord your God with all your heart, and with all your soul, and with all your strength, and with all your mind; and your neighbour as yourself.' And he said to him, 'You have given the right answer; do this, and you will live.'*
>
> *Luke 10:27-28*

He answered, 'You shall love'...

Jesus deliberately asked the lawyer what is in the law? Yet Jesus was not referring to any law, but the law of the Great Commandment, because it all comes down to love. That is the only answer.

The lawyer is asking, 'What must I do to inherit eternal life?' Jesus is telling him it is not about doing. You can neither work for, nor inherit eternal life. It is not achieved by our merits. It is far from earning indulgences or doing great things. It is a path of discovery that occurs through God's grace. Jesus is leading the lawyer off the beaten track, down a different path, away from worthiness and success, to a hidden path where we may come to know that only love matters. 'You shall love', and in that experience your path is illuminated before you, the path to truth, to joy, to deep prayer, the path to eternal life.

'You shall love' is a coming-to action. It is not an imperative, 'you must'. Rather, it is a direction you choose to take, the direction of love. You shall… You shall come to love… you shall come to know the truth. All in good time.

'You shall love.' You will one day learn and embrace the art of love. When you fall into the love of God and when you become love itself, it takes over your heart, soul, strength and mind, and then you will know what is eternal life.

'You shall love' is more than a request or plea or option. It is something integral to who we are. Love is what God is and our coming to God can only be through love. Any other knowing of God is less. God has to be ultimate, greater than us, immeasurable, uncontainable, for that is what love alone is.

The crux of it all is that everyone can inherit eternal life. 'You shall' is a possibility for everyone, as it is not based on our deeds, experiences, wealth or knowledge. 'You shall' is a promise to each and every person. 'You shall' is hope filled, promising each one of us that there will come a time when we shall know what love is, we shall know God with our whole being, we shall love completely, we shall see one another through eyes of love and we shall have eternal life when we know love. 'You shall love' is a capacity we all have.

'You shall love.' It is to come to the knowledge, the understanding, the insight, to the belief, to faith, to conclusion, that there is a God, something beyond my ego, something greater than I. The 'I am who I am' (Exodus 3:14).

'You shall love.' It is a promise. That is and will remain the greatest commandment and ultimate claim on our lives.

He answered, 'You shall love the Lord your God with all your heart, and with all your soul, and with all your strength, and with all your mind'.

The lawyer knows the answer to his own question and provides the response by quoting Deuteronomy 6:5, 'You shall love the Lord your God with all your heart, and with all your soul, and with all your might'. However, the full *Shema* quote in Deuteronomy 6:4-9 that every Jew was to follow was:

> Hear, O Israel: The Lord is our God, the Lord alone. You shall love the Lord your God with all your heart, and with all your soul, and with all your might. Keep these words that I am

commanding you today in your heart. Recite them to your children and talk about them when you are at home and when you are away, when you lie down and when you rise. Bind them as a sign on your hand, fix them as an emblem on your forehead, and write them on the doorposts of your house and on your gates.

'You shall love the Lord' is a statement of life commitment to God; and faithfulness to a relationship with him. It is to 'act lovingly toward' or 'to honour and be loyal to'. Rabbinic thought of Jesus' time embraced the idea that salvation came by faith rather than by works. They understood that the relationship with God must always come first, and only after we have that, do we obey God's commandments.[6]

Yet, inheriting eternal life is about Torah commands put into action. Eternal life is not to be secured through faith, belief, rituals or one's ethnic status alone. It is neither duty, nor earned. It is about engaging the heart, soul, strength and mind. It is about loving God and ourselves and others.

To love God is to find ourselves on the edge, to differ in understanding, to go against the flow. It calls us out of our complacency, our comfort zone. It just unravels everything we had neatly tidied away. It shakes

---

6 Lois Tverberg, *Jesus' Surprising Answer* 5 June 2019. https://engediresourcecenter.com/2019/06/05/jesus-surprising-answer/

us up, calls us to do things we would rather turn a blind eye to, or remain ignorant about because ignorance is bliss! It calls us to be like God, which is very different to what we are comfortable with.

> For my thoughts are not your thoughts, nor are your ways my ways, says the Lord. For as the heavens are higher than the earth, so are my ways higher than your ways and my thoughts than your thoughts. (Isaiah 55:8-9)

As it is, we live in a world very unlike what God asks of us. Love is not understood in the way God loves us. Love today is romanticised. It is about indulgence, the flesh, spending leisurely time with another. So for many, when they hear the term love of God, it strikes fear, or apathy, or distaste. It is too much effort to love God. To love God feels distant and cold, it takes effort and time, and we would rather be thinking or doing something else more to our liking, something that offers sensual satisfaction. Then there is the bigger problem of how we are meant to love a God we cannot see or hear or, more importantly, touch! And if we cannot touch or see or hear, how do we even know there is a God worth loving anyway?

To love God is, first, to have experienced God's love. There needs to be a personal encounter. The knowing of God, accepting there is a God, to love God, revolves around our closeness and ongoing relationship with God. Our image of who God is plays a leading role in the kind of relationship we have with God. Stern images do not assist in enabling a loving relationship. A God of tenderness and compassion make the Torah command so much easier, as the following suggests:

> Then the Lord said, 'I have observed the misery of my people who are in Egypt; I have heard their cry on account of their taskmasters. Indeed, I know their sufferings, and I have come down to deliver them from the Egyptians, and to bring them up out of that land to a good and broad land, a land flowing with milk and honey'. (Exodus 3:7-8)

> You have seen what I did to the Egyptians, and how I bore you on eagles' wings and brought you to myself. (Exodus 19:4)

> Can a woman forget her nursing child, or show no compassion for the child of her womb? Even these may forget, yet I will not forget you. (Isaiah 49:15)

> But now thus says the Lord, he who created you, O Jacob, he who formed you, O Israel: Do not fear, for I have redeemed you; I have called you by name, you are mine... Because you are precious in my sight, and honoured, and I love you,

I give people in return for you, nations in exchange for your life. (Isaiah 43:1, 4)

Yet it was I who taught Ephraim to walk, I took them up in my arms; but they did not know that I healed them. I led them with cords of human kindness, with bands of love. I was to them like those who lift infants to their cheeks. I bent down to them and fed them. (Hosea 11:3-4)

When I look at your heavens, the work of your fingers, the moon and the stars that you have established; what are human beings that you are mindful of them, mortals that you care for them? (Psalm 8:3-4)

But you do see! Indeed you note trouble and grief, that you may take it into your hands; the helpless commit themselves to you; you have been the helper of the orphan. (Psalm 10:14)

In Jesus, we can be assured that God commits to humanity, God loves people, God works miracles, God knows suffering. It is a God who dies for us. This is the God we are called to love with our entire being and it is only to such a self-giving God can we truly give our love.

So our lives are not simply to study or admire Jesus from a distance. We are called to a deeper knowing of Christ in order that we may become like him and follow his ways. If we say Jesus is love, compassion, God's Son, or our Redeemer, it means we must be responsive to Jesus in a way consistent with our understanding. We must take on board these very characteristics we extol in Jesus.

To love God is a movement of the heart, a searching of the mind, an awakening of the spirit. In 1 Corinthians 2:16 we read, 'For who has known the mind of the Lord so as to instruct him? But we have the mind of Christ'. It is to give our entire being to loving God. To exercise the heart, soul, strength and mind in engagement with God is meant to be our one focus, and it should influence everything else we do. It means every thought, every action, every moment, we turn and face God. Our motives, inspirations, decisions, words, behaviour, the very being of who we are, our character and image, become God's.

It is to be open, vulnerable, ready, accessible, willing, empty, in need, searching, hoping, yearning, patient, waiting, silent, deeply needing, wanting, present, attentive, awakened, aware, perceiving, expecting, delighting, in joy and in sorrow, in light and in dark – totally there to God. God demands all of us. Can we give all of ourselves to God and thus say with Paul, 'It is no longer I who live, but it is Christ who lives in me' (Galatians 2:20).

... and your neighbour as yourself...

Interestingly, the lawyer further quotes Leviticus 19:18, 'You shall love your neighbour as yourself'. He did not need to add this line but does so, wanting to prove his in-depth knowledge of the law and possibly his sincerity in seeking an answer to his question.

'Love your neighbour as yourself' from Leviticus 19:18 has a rare word, *ve'ahavta*, meaning 'and you shall love' in common with that of words of the *Shema* that shows total commitment to God, 'And you shall love the Lord your God.' The way to express total love and commitment to God, whom we cannot see, was by showing love to neighbour, whom we can see.

First century understanding was that loving your neighbour was the clearest expression of your commitment to God. So the lawyer gave the best possible answer, using first century Jewish terminology, to say that we need to commit ourselves to the Lord and live our faith out wholeheartedly. And Jesus responds, 'Yes, do this!'

In directing the lawyer to the law and affirming his response, Jesus indicates that the key to inheriting eternal life is to be found in obeying the Torah commandments. It is to love God and neighbour. Ethical action is all that matters, a point Jesus emphasises in the only two answers he offers the lawyer, 'Do this and you will live' in verse 28 and, 'Go and do likewise' in verse 37.[7]

This teaching on love of neighbour continues throughout the New Testament. Jesus says, 'No one has greater love than this, to lay down one's life for one's friends' (John 15:13). Peter writes, 'above all, love one another' (1 Peter 4:8), and in the First Letter of John, we read, 'this was the teaching you have heard from the very beginning – to love one another' (1 John 3:11). Paul also eloquently writes about love in his First Letter to the Corinthians:

> Love is patient; love is kind; love is not envious or boastful or arrogant or rude. It does not insist on its own way; it is not irritable or resentful; it does not rejoice in wrongdoing, but rejoices in the truth. It bears all things, believes all things, hopes all things, endures all things. Love never ends. (1 Corinthians 13:4-8)

Yet, if the lawyer must follow the law to love God and neighbour, it may prove difficult if your neighbour is your enemy! But maybe, just perhaps, the neighbour is not an enemy as assumed. Maybe God's law and human law differ. Do we really know God's demands on us, or have we misinterpreted God, manipulated God,

---

[7] Lois Tverberg, *Jesus' Surprising Answer* 5 June 2019.
https://engediresourcecenter.com/2019/06/05/jesus-surprising-answer/

used God, to put into place barriers and arguments, defences and fences, laws and decrees that are most convenient to us?

Thomas H. Groome notes that our partnership with one another actualises our partnership with God. The human condition is realised as a community-of-persons. We are always person-in-community. Our human identity is first and foremost relational; we become who we are through relationship with other people.[8] This may be one of the most important insights we gained during the 2020 Covid-19 imposed lockdown and self-isolation. People felt the yearning to be with others, to love their neighbour!

The *Universal Declaration of Human Rights* encompasses a great deal of what the parable of the Good Samaritan teaches. If you run your eyes down the list of thirty articles, you will find a number of these echoed in the parable. Below are a select few which could be considered practical applications to 'love of neighbour':[9]

- Article 1: All human beings are born free and equal in dignity and rights. They are endowed with reason and conscience and

---

[8] Thomas H. Groome, *What makes us Catholic. Eight gifts for life.* (NY: HarperSanFrancisco, 2002), 60.

[9] The Universal Declaration of Human Rights. 2015 United Nations.

https://www.un.org/en/udhrbook/pdf/udhr_booklet_en_web.pdf

should act towards one another in a spirit of brotherhood.

- Article 2: Everyone is entitled to all the rights and freedoms set forth in this Declaration, without distinction of any kind, such as race, colour, sex, language, religion, political or other opinion, national or social origin, property, birth or other status. Furthermore, no distinction shall be made on the basis of the political, jurisdictional or international status of the country or territory to which a person belongs, whether it be independent, trust, non-self-governing or under any other limitation of sovereignty.
- Article 5: No one shall be subjected to torture or to cruel, inhuman or degrading treatment or punishment.

In preparation for the 2020/2021 Australian Catholic Plenary Council, people were asked the question, 'What do you think God is asking of us in Australia at this time?' One of the most common answers was, 'to love God and love neighbour'. There were a significant number of responses calling for greater love, kindness, respect and care for our neighbours.[10]

---

[10] Trudy Dantis, Paul Bowell, Stephen Reid and LethDudfield, *Listen to what the Spirit is saying. Final Report for the Plenary Council. Phase 1: Listening and Dialogue,* (National Centre for Pastoral Research, Australian Catholic Bishops Conference,

Purpose of the journey

They also expressed a need and responsibility for helping everyone without disregarding the needs of any one group:

> God is asking us to treat each other as we would like to be treated, with kindness and respect. That includes every person we directly or indirectly encounter, refugees, homeless on the street, colleagues, family members, everyone. As members of the Catholic Church, we should take this message everywhere.[11]

These are just a few examples of the universal application of the teachings of the parable of the Good Samaritan, a story told over 2000 years ago, but with an essential message for all humanity.

And he said to him, 'You have given the right answer; do this, and you will live.'

Jesus does not say to do this and you will inherit eternal life. He says, do this and you will live. Jesus is indicating what to do now for the sake of now, not what to do now

---

2019), 28.
https://plenarycouncil.catholic.org.au/wp-content/uploads/2019/09/FINAL-BOOK-v7-online-version-LISTEN-TO-WIIAT-THE SPIRIT-IS-SAYING.pdf

11 Dantis, *Listen to what the Spirit is saying. Final Report for the Plenary Council. Phase 1: Listening and Dialogue,'* 36.

for the sake of tomorrow and eternal life. Eckhart Tolle writes:

> Yet on a deeper level you are already complete, and when you realise that, there is a playful, joyous energy behind what you do. Being free of psychological time, you no longer pursue your goals with grim determination, driven by fear, anger, discontent, or the need to become someone...
> Everything is honoured, but nothing matters. Forms are born and die, yet you are aware of the eternal underneath the forms...
> On the level of form, you share mortality and the precariousness of existence. On the level of Being, you share eternal, radiant life.[12]

To live is to live in the now, to be present to the present. Jesus is encouraging the lawyer neither to worry about tomorrow nor yesterday, but to live now, for that is all we really have and what really matters.

Following from this parable, a little further on in Luke's Gospel we read how Jesus emphasises the present, 'And can any of you by worrying add a single hour to your span of life?' (Luke 12:25). The simple answer is no!

All too often we are pursuing the future, waiting for tomorrow, or mourning the past. Yet life is right

---

[12] Eckhart Tolle, *The Power of Now. A guide to spiritual enlightenment.* (California: New World Library, 2004), 69, 70, 197.

here, right now, where we are. It is what happens now and today that will shape tomorrow and determine the future. So eternal life is life now. It is what we do with what we have been given that counts. 'You will live' Jesus tells the lawyer, and indeed you will truly live when you can enjoy the moment and when you are ready to fully embrace this life with wonder.

Chapter 3

Companions on the journey

> *But wanting to justify himself, he asked Jesus, 'And who is my neighbour?'*
>
> Luke 10:29

But wanting to justify himself...

If the right answer to the lawyer's question was, 'You shall love the Lord your God with all your heart, and with all your soul, and with all your strength, and with your entire mind; and your neighbour as yourself' (v. 27), then why persist on probing further? Surely, that resolves any further questioning.

Yet loving humanity as a whole is more easily achieved than to love your neighbour. So the lawyer tries to limit the parametres of the law by asking the question 'who is my neighbour?' Charles de Foucauld notes:

From the moment in which we begin to judge anyone, to limit our confidence in them, from the moment at which we identify the person with what we know of them and so reduce them to that, we cease to love the person and they cease to be able to become better. We should expect everything of everyone. We must dare to be love in a world that does not know how to love.

The lawyer commenced with a question. However, this is followed through with another question and his real intentions are revealed. As Amy-Jill Levine notes, to ask 'Who is my neighbour?' is a polite way of asking, 'Who is not my neighbour?' or 'Who does not deserve my love?' or 'Whom I can hate?' The answer Jesus gives, to the lawyer's disappointment is, 'No one'.[13]

We ask questions, not to know the deeper truth, but to niggle and annoy and frustrate the other. And sadly we get drawn into petty squabbles, endless interrogation, digging up the past, doubts and insinuations, all in the effort to justify ourselves, as we masquerade behind the law and so-called justice.

Jesus is not guilty of any wrongdoing, but because he challenged assumptions and rocked the *status quo*, he became a target. Opposition and critics occur in

---

[13] Amy-Jill Levine, *Go and Do Likewise: Lessons from the parable of the Good Samaritan,* 17 September 17 2014https://www.americamagazine.org/faith/2014/09/17/go-and-do-likewise-lessons-parable-good-samaritan

life and they can come out of the blue, unexpectedly. We are never left in peace. In today's society, anyone and everyone can become a target for someone else's agenda. We all are someone else's scapegoat, stalked by trolls intent on virtual attack. Whether we are innocent or not, once the challenge is given, we must respond and, unfortunately, the game of cat and mouse can follow and become very intimidating. Intentions are revealed and all too often they are not honourable.

The hate agenda, especially against people of faith, can be relentless and unmerciful. Such opponents hide under the barrier of justice of the law, but they harbour a darker desire, and pursue whatever means they have to destroy the one they hound. It might be worthwhile here to pause and reflect on our own behaviour:

> What in our lives are we condemned for?
> Does our truth stand strong in the face of torment?
> What do we base our sense of justice on?
> What clouds our decision-making?
> Why are we so insistent on justifying ourselves?
> What is the intention behind our questions?
> Who is the victim?
> Who do we accuse and abuse in our lives?

Like the lawyer, we are so quick to play the blame game, to be judge and executioner, to distort meaning for our own justification, to demonise those who threaten our credibility, to turn our evil intent into good deeds by claiming it is for the better good of others. We gather more fuel for our intentions by garnering the support of others. Then we take a stance that upholds the image of ourselves that we want others to see and believe, and we do all it takes to defend that image, even if others must get hurt along the way. We forego principles and sacrifice truth in our relentless and destructive pursuit of justifying ourselves. For where there is absence of love, mercy and forgiveness, nothing can flourish.

We should neither be able to simply mock another's deep convictions, nor to shut out and silence truth.

Pilate asks, 'What is truth?' (John 18:38). He is like so many others who pose questions to hide behind them, rather than to unlock the truth. Where can anyone receive a fair hearing when the very law meant to protect their basic rights is made a mockery of by the justice system? Basic rights denied in a web of lies. It is a mock trial. There are unwitting scapegoats. Truth is dissected and left in tatters. Hands are washed clean. No accountability. No justice. No truth. And Jesus, along with many others, pays with his life to appease authorities intent on wielding their power, at the expense of anyone who opposes them or offers a different view.

People want to do away with truth and they will stop at nothing. The world promotes lies. Those who hold power manipulate, destroy and obliterate anything to do with Jesus, and they do it relentlessly, mercilessly. They wield the power of the media, the courtrooms, the defence force and the politicians.

Perhaps the lawyer and many of us who want to justify ourselves and make a mockery of another by hiding behind laws should heed the words of George Eliot:

> All people of broad strong sense have an instinctive repugnance to the men of maxims; because such people early discern that the mysterious complexity of our life is not to be embraced by maxims, and that to lace ourselves up in formulas of that sort is to repress all the divine promptings and inspirations that spring from growing insight and sympathy. And the man of maxims is the popular representatives of the minds that are guided in their moral judgment solely by general rules, thinking that these will lead them to justice by a ready-made method, without the trouble of exerting patience, discrimination, impartiality, without any care to assure themselves whether they have the insight that comes from a hardly-earned estimate of temptation, or from a life vivid and intense enough to have created a wide fellow-feeling with all that is human.[14]

---

14 George Eliot, *The Mill on the Floss*, (London: Penguin Classics, 1979), 628.

Condemnation, passing judgment, to be told, 'You are guilty', labelled a liar, untrustworthy, bad, evil, a wrong doer – such accusations blows apart our self esteem, our reality. It is wrong and hurtful.

So what response do we give? Where do we turn to for a fair go? For our human dignity to be recognised? For our survival? This is where God becomes essential, for truth cannot be heard in the hands of fickle people, neither through courtrooms nor the media, as they have proven to be unreliable and easily manipulated. Truth will prevail through God, in God's time.

Jesus was astute in claiming we are 'like sheep in the midst of wolves', but Jesus was also streetwise enough to suggest that we 'be wise as serpents and innocent as doves' (Matthew 10:16). We are neither to remain submissive nor play the naïve victim. A response is demanded from us, but we are never to lose our integrity.

There will always be people who demand the truth be bared, told, publicly made known. Otherwise life is an endless cycle of lies not worth living. Truth matters and it is what gives us meaning, purpose and hope, for it allows the best use of our strength, for putting our virtues into action.

Nothing will stop evil, and yet nothing will stop God either. God cannot be killed off. God cannot be got rid of. God cannot be denied and silenced. God will be tested but not found wanting, judged but not found guilty.

... he asked Jesus, 'And who is my neighbour?'

So who is my neighbour? The word 'neighbour' in Greek means 'someone who is near' and in Hebrew it means 'someone that you have an association with'. This interprets the word in a limited sense, referring to a fellow Jew and excluding Samaritans, Romans and other foreigners.[15] Perhaps a better definition is the example Anthony J. Gittins provides:

> 'When do you know it is dawn?' asked the rabbi. One person said, 'When you can see a tree against the horizon'. 'No', said the rabbi. Someone else said, 'When you can distinguish a black thread from a white one'. 'No', he answered again. And when no one else had an answer, the rabbi said: 'When you can look into the face of a stranger and recognise your brother or your sister; then you know it is dawn. Until then, it is still night'.[16]

So then is our neighbour the very least, or the stranger, or do we just want to brag about knowing the rich and famous? All too often we limit the understanding of neighbour to our family, relatives, friends, work colleagues, church community, sporting

---

15 'What is the meaning of the Parable of the Good Samaritan?' in *Got Questions. Your Questions. Biblical Answers.* https://www.gotquestions.org/parable-Good-Samaritan.html

16 Anthony J. Gittins, *Called to be sent. Co-missioned as disciples today,* (Oregon: Wipf and Stock, 2008), 137.

mates and street neighbours. Or we can at times be like Jonah the prophet who questions why help the ones we despise?

> When God saw what they did, how they turned from their evil ways, God changed his mind about the calamity that he had said he would bring upon them; and he did not do it. But this was very displeasing to Jonah, and he became angry. (Jonah 3:10 to 4:1)

Our neighbour can be anyone, even if we wish to think otherwise or argue that they do not deserve it. In the Sermon on the Plain, Jesus says, 'Love your enemies, do good to those who hate you, bless those who curse you, pray for those who mistreat you' (Luke 6:27–28). So there are two ways to understand the question, 'Who is my neighbour?' It can be:

- The neighbour in need, which has been the traditional way of understanding the question.
- The neighbour who approaches the one in need, which is a more challenging understanding of the question, because the onus is back on us.

The neighbour in need:

- Who do we recognise as requiring assistance?

- When does the stranger become our neighbour?

The neighbour as the one who approaches another in need:

- To what lengths do I go in my care for others?
- Who are the people my heart goes out to and I give my time for?

It might be of value to remember the famous quote by John Donne:

> No man is an island, entire of itself;
> Every man is a piece of the continent, a part of the main.
> If a clod be washed away by the sea,
> Europe is the less.
> As well as if a promontory were.
> As well as if a manor of thy friend's or of thine own were:
> Any man's death diminishes me,
> Because I am involved in mankind,
> And therefore never send to know for whom the bell tolls;
> It tolls for thee.[17]

---

17 John Donne, 'Meditation XVII,' in *Devotions upon Emergent Occasions,* 1623.

So putting the two perspectives side by side, is being a neighbour therefore:

1) The person in need? OR

2) The one who offers care?

OR is it both?

The lawyer seeks to learn from Jesus the identity of the one whom he was required to love as himself. Instead, the parable provides an example of a nameless compassionate Samaritan as being identified as the neighbour.

Jesus changes the focus of the word 'neighbour' away from a recipient of love as in Leviticus 19:18, 'love your neighbour' to the person who does the loving, 'Which of these three was a neighbour to the man who fell into the hands of the robbers?' There is neither friend nor foe. We are all just friends, neighbours to one another.

'Who is my neighbour?' Many ask this question hoping for a response that some people are not. Instead, this parable turns the question on its head. We are called to be a neighbour whenever we are needed and to recognise that neighbours can come from surprising places.[18]

---

[18] Jeff Bloem, *An Economist Takes on the Parable of the Good Samaritan,* April 27, 2017

https://jeffbloem.wordpress.com/2017/04/27/an-economist-takes-on-the-parable-of-the-good-samaritan/

Yet being a neighbour can cost us. To be a neighbour to the unexpected stranger can be threatening for both parties, but we need to remember, just because God is for us and with us, God is not against others. Even if we struggle to be a neighbour to others – and we will surely struggle at times – at least we should not resort to making them our enemy. Jesus invites the lawyer to let go of the game of self-justification and focus on the other, for that is where answers to our questions lie.

So who is my neighbour? Surely not every person whose path crosses mine! Surely not every person in need that I encounter? Surely not the stranger or the enemy? Surely not.

A neighbour cannot be out there. The neighbour includes the people around us, here in our local vicinity. And yet here we have the parable of the Good Samaritan and the neighbour ends up being a stranger, on a distant road.

The world has become much smaller, the distance between people has narrowed. We have become a global village quite literally. In the past, foreigners were looked upon with suspicion and religion was segregating. Today, with our easy access to world travel, no one is a foreigner, and religion is one of many choices. We live in a world that we travel through, where we are meant to come to know one another, greet one another and assist one another on the way. We are invited to be open and accepting of one another's differences as we cross each other's paths in this global village.

Maybe, though, it does start at home. Maybe we must first acknowledge our neighbour over the fence. We first need to learn how to look over the fence and greet our neighbour. Can we exchange polite words, discuss the weather, maybe even offer some homemade cooking? Once we can scale the fences between us at a local level, we will find it easier to hurdle bigger barriers between us on a national level and then be open enough to others on an international level.

Chapter 4

The journey begins with trouble on the horizon

> *Jesus replied, 'A man was going down from Jerusalem to Jericho and fell into the hands of robbers who stripped him, beat him, and went away, leaving him half dead.*
>
> Luke 10:30

Jesus replied...

Jesus' favourite speech form, the parable, was subversive. It was a great piece of storytelling with a twist! He continually threw odd stories down alongside ordinary lives (*para* 'alongside'; *bole* 'thrown') and walked away without explanation. Parables sound ordinary: casual stories about soil and seeds, meals and coins and sheep, bandits and victims, farmers and merchants, elaborates Eugene H. Peterson. As people heard Jesus tell these stories, they saw at once that they were not about God, so there was nothing in them threatening. The listeners relaxed their defences and walked away, wondering what they meant. The parables put the listener's imagination to work, which if they were not careful, would become the exercise of faith. Parables subversively slip past defences while integrity is honoured and preserved.[19]

William J. Bausch delineated six characteristics of the New Testament parables:

- They uncover our competitiveness and envy and invite us to brotherhood and sisterhood.
- They uncover our wrong centring and invite us to a right centring.
- They uncover our need to hoard and exclude and invite us to share and include.
- They uncover our assumptions and challenge us to turn them around.
- They uncover our timidity and invite us to risk all for the sake of God's kingdom.
- They uncover our self-centred despair and distrust and invite us to hope.[20]

---

19 Eugene H. Peterson, *The Contemplative Pastor. Returning to the Art of Spiritual Direction,* (Grand Rapids, Michigan: William B. Eerdmans Publishing Company, 1989), 32-33.

20 William J. Bausch, *Storytelling: Imagination and Faith* (Mystic, CT: Twenty-Third Publications, 1984), 117-137.

The purpose of parables differs from straightforward instructional genres such as commandments, rules and procedures. Parables involve provoking a playful but serious labour of interpretation, an opening to possibilities of meaning, rather than indicating a single denotation.[21] Perhaps that is why Jesus not only turns the lawyer's focus to the law, but challenges him further through the telling of a parable.

Jesus' teaching through parables can be viewed as monologic, subversive 'codifications' that challenge the political and economic status quo, concerned with the transformation of enculturated consciousness and conventional morality.[22] So Jesus used parables to illuminate the flaws in his society and in those who determined its course. The parables thus are not merely innocent stories about God in relation to individual humans. Rather, they proclaim God's will in relation to a particular human society whose members they confront with standards of justice that challenge that society to change.[23]

---

21 Rule, P. N., 'The pedagogy of Jesus in the parable of the Good Samaritan: A diacognitive analysis', *HTS Teologiese Studies/ Theological Studies* 73(3), 2017:2. https://doi.org/10.4102/hts.v73i3.3886

22 Rule, 'The pedagogy of Jesus in the parable of the Good Samaritan: A diacognitive analysis,' 1.

23 R. David Kaylor, *Jesus the Prophet. His Vision of the Kingdom on Earth*, (Louisville, Kentucky: Westminster/John Knox Press, 1994), 128.

The journey begins with trouble on the horizon

A man was going down from Jerusalem to Jericho...

The lawyer was asking about eternal life and Jesus commences the parable with a Jew leaving Jerusalem to head to Jericho. Jerusalem was meant to be the eternal holy city, the place where God resides in the Temple. Yet this man is leaving the eternal city for another place. Maybe to receive eternal life we need to leave our comfort zone, our false understanding of God and search more widely. God is not only in the Temple, but waits for us on the road called life. It is to go outside, out of our narrow confines, off the beaten track, in order to experience life with others. Through our daily encounters we are better prepared for life eternal with God.

Jericho was well irrigated and lush, earning the title, 'City of a Thousand Palms'. Many priests had their homes in Jericho. Jerusalem, in contrast, was in the hill country (800m above sea level), while Jericho was on a plain (250m below sea level). The road that goes down from Jerusalem to Jericho is 25 kilometres long and passes through a deserted area. It is treacherously winding and hazardous, becoming a hideout of robbers and thieves. People travelled this route in caravans for protection, and yet the parable tells of those travelling alone.

Like the road from Jerusalem to Jericho, there are treacherous, long roads we have to take alone in life. There are risks and arduous journeys. We know the possible dangers, yet we take the decision to go on, with the hope that all will be well.

So what have been our roads of hazard? Is it the next neighbourhood? Our workplace? Has it been dealing with death, illness, whistle blowing or bullying? The road of life is not always smooth travelling. There will be scenic routes, but also potholes, blockades, curves and wrong turns. Yet, to veer off our course, to make a detour, to move from our comfort zone, is always a risk. The road ahead may be perilous and fraught with danger. Many wish to harm, others sidestep and only a few come to aid.

On hazardous or arduous journeys, there are times we so equip ourselves with padding and defence mechanisms that we never really experience the troubles on the road. Then there are times we come with our propaganda, rhetoric, high morals, principles and philosophies, that we come and go without really having experienced a difference, or more so, we come and go, having made things worse for others.

On our journey in life, do we do what has to be done, or are we far more concerned about our own safety? Do we go to distant places, on long and dangerous journeys, to conquer or to save and redeem others, who do not need a salvation that condemns but a salvation that cares?

Pope Francis writes in *Evangelii Gaudium* that 'Face-to-face encounter with others, with their physical

The journey begins with trouble on the horizon

presence which challenges us' (*EG* 88), is necessary as is, 'Drawing near to forms of poverty and vulnerability' (*EG* 210). In our journey, our travellings, our ministry, we need to examine what message and attitude we carry with us towards others.

Taking another perspective, in our travelling, we would do well to reflect not only on the attitude we have when journeying, but the how and with whom, we choose to travel. In the parable, one man was walking on his own. And then there is the priest walking on his own. And the Levite walking on his own. And the Samaritan walking on his own. Sometimes we must take the solitary walk on our journey. The how of the journey matters. It gives us time to reflect, to take in the view, to reconnect with God. If we use quiet time wisely, then we are better prepared when we come across strangers on our road. How we respond to them is determined by how we spent our solitary journey.

We plough the seas, reach out to the universe, climb heights and peer into microscopes. Yet, the very journey of adventure that matters most and reveals the greatest wonders and truths is that inner journey to our heart, the soul searching, that guides us on the right path. So where are we heading?

The path ever lies before us and entices us deeper and further in. There is a curiosity for life, to keep going, to see where it will lead us, to find that inner sanctum where we truly reach a destination worth the travel. But it is always about the journey, the continual movement, with its wonderful sights, its experiences of ups and downs, its unexpected twists and turns. As Mary MacKillop reflected in 1909, 'Remember we are but travelers here'.

So enough is enough. There is no more time for delay, for tardiness, for procrastination, for excuses, for self-pity, for disabling fear. Life is here and now at our doorstep. It passes with all its promises and hardships. Do we step out of our comfort zone and step onto the road of life? It is time to walk out and walk on. To see what lies ahead of us. To walk beyond our own narrow vision into a larger world. To see things differently, discover a new world, meet all sorts of people, to lend a helping hand, to smell the roses, to join in solidarity with the downtrodden, to do what has to be done. Life is not about self-preservation but self-exploration.

Even if we start the journey with the wrong direction and turn off roads and go via other detours, Jesus walks with us. As they say, all roads lead to Rome. We can find our way home. There will be forks in the road, better decisions to be made, short cuts ahead. We can get to where we want to be, where answers to our questions are found, as long as we keep moving on, looking ahead, being attentive to the signs on our road of life. The red lights, the stop signs, the U turns, the dead ends, the roundabouts, they all ask us to slow down and take heed of our surroundings. In doing so, they point us to a new direction, another way, a path not noticed in our previous speed, encouraging us to get off the beaten track and to forge a new way ahead.

... and fell...

There are those that prey on others, intent on their downfall. Today we witness, as we have throughout history, those who fall victim to the evil intentions of others. Drug addiction and drug mules because they had fallen into the hands of underworld people. Child labour, modern day slavery and prostitution because they had fallen into the hands of crime lords.

To fall is to say that those who find themselves thrown into a dark world are often unwitting and unwilling victims. It is not through their own decisions, but a falling, a slipping away, an exposure to an unfortunate set of events. It can be the notion of falling into, a giving up of themselves, or a practice in vulnerability.

The term 'spiralling down' is apt. There are times we have no control and we feel like we are plunged head first into disaster. We have mixed with the wrong set of people and found ourselves being dragged into deeper and darker places. As Paul writes in 1 Corinthians 15:33, 'Bad company ruins good morals'. Like the beaten man in the parable, there comes a time where we have fallen so low, hit rock bottom, that it takes a miracle to get us out.

Yet, we die small deaths each day and in our daily dying, we experience also daily risings. In our fallen state, we begin to understand how important it is to get back up, to seek out others who can help us, no matter who they are. Nothing is achieved on the bottom, but the will to get up. It is not in our nature to stay down and be kicked around.

The miracle is God's grace, found in the presence of another who chooses to be in the image of God. We can neither walk through life unscathed, nor without companionship. Life will deal its blows but it will also offer a helping hand. Madame Jeanne Guyon notes:

> If knowing answers to life's questions is absolutely necessary to you, then forget the journey. You will never make it, for this is a journey of unknowables – of unanswered questions, enigmas, incomprehensible, and most of all, things unfair.[24]

Are we the fallen one? Or the one to raise the fallen at this moment in our journey? We do not know what circumstances we will find ourselves in, nor our loved ones. It reminds us of the Scriptural quote:

---

[24] Jeanne Guyon, *Experiencing the depths of Jesus Christ. One of the greatest Christian writings of all time. Library of Spiritual Classics. Vol 2.* (US: SeedSowers, Christian Books Publishing House, 1975).

The journey begins with trouble on the horizon

Then David said to Gad, 'I am in great distress; let us fall into the hand of the Lord, for his mercy is great; but let me not fall into human hands'. (2 Samuel 24:14)

To fall into God's hand requires vulnerability and humility but with the assurance that we will be raised again, unlike falling into human hands.

How many of us lie gutted, fallen, depressed, in need of a helping hand, a kind word, a gentle presence? But there is no one around to care. Yet we urgently need someone to care. As Scripture says, 'Ask the Lord of the harvest to send out labourers into his harvest' (Luke 10:2). Hurting people are many but healing people are wanting. We need love, desperately. We are the beaten person. We are hurting, fallen, abandoned, devastated. Can love be enfleshed? Can hope become a reality? Nothing else is in greater demand.

We fall, stumble, trip and lose our balance in life. What knocks us down, pushes us to our knees, rubs our face in the dirt? There are pains and sorrows, sickness and ill health, shame and guilt, depression and isolation, enemies and opposition, hurts and losses, failures and weaknesses.

Yet despite our downfall, we have the Paschal Mystery and we take comfort and strength in knowing that what happens to Christ happens to us. It is to have total reliance on grace in our weakness. From there new life can grow. Remember, the very beginnings of

Christianity emerged from the trauma at the Cross, but then it flourished.

... and fell into the hands of robbers...

The man was beaten and left for dead and we too may be fine one day, but a neighbour in desperate need the next. A person can be going about their business and suddenly become the unexpected victim of violence, terror or horror. There are so many instances of injustice and brutality, and so many that are hushed up, hidden or ignored.

Who do we become victim to?

Are we involved in acts of hatred and violence?

Who is our prey?

Who are the robbers and thieves today?

Not named, but anyone who strips others of their dignity and self-sufficiency can be considered a robber. They might not be so visible as in our Gospel passage, but it is anyone who robs from others – their identity, security, possessions, pride, opportunities, reputation.

We try desperately not to be captured by the mindset and lifestyle of hedonists, people who cast God aside for their own adulation, and yet we can see it all around us, the infiltration of a society through promotion of selfish, lustful desires. And there are so many cries which echo down through the centuries that we ignore:

The journey begins with trouble on the horizon

Millions massacred
Civilisations destroyed
Nations at war
Senseless killings
Bloodbaths
Terrorist attacks
Violent crimes
Depraved acts
Demeaning of the human
Distortion of principles
Valueless society
Sadistic mentality
Promiscuity
Erosion of any sense of dignity, culture, faith, meaning and morals

As we witness to injustice and suffering, we wonder how we could be made in God's image and how possible it is to stray so far away. Yet Michael Tubbs notes:

> We've been focused on the robbers and the road. So in Stockton, as I mentioned, we have historically had problems with violent crime. And my first job as mayor was helping our community to see ourselves, our neighbours, not just in the people victimized by violence but also in the perpetrators. We

realized that those who enact pain in our society, those who are committing homicides and contributing to gun violence, are oftentimes victims themselves. They have high rates of trauma, they have been shot at, they've known people who have been shot. That doesn't excuse their behaviour, but it helps explain it, and as a community, we have to see these folks as us, too. That they too are our neighbours.[25]

It is a thought worth giving extensive consideration to. Who is my neighbour – the one that causes me harm, can they too be my neighbour? If so, where did it all go so wrong? Leo Tolstoy writes in *War and Peace*, 'It seemed to him that he had been vicious only because he had somehow forgotten how good it is to be virtuous'.[26]

So if we turned our gaze to the robbers, what will we see before our very eyes? Perhaps we may come to realise their motivation arose from desperation – perhaps for money they were unable to gain through acceptable means. Yet all have the right to a financially secure life and to be able to meet their basic needs. The United Nations Declaration of Human Rights articles 22 and 23 encapsulate what Jesus taught:

---

25 Michael Tubbs, *The political power of being a good neighbor* TED Talk, April 2019.
https://www.ted.com/talks/michael_tubbs_the_political_power_of_being_a_good_neighbor
26 Leo Tolstoy, *War and Peace,* Trans. Louise and Aylmer Maude, (Oxford: Oxford University Press, 2010), 378.

- Article 22: Everyone, as a member of society, has the right to social security and is entitled to realisation, through national effort and international cooperation and in accordance with the organisation and resources of each State, of the economic, social and cultural rights indispensable for his dignity and the free development of his personality.

- Article 23: (1) Everyone has the right to work, to free choice of employment, to just and favourable conditions of work and to protection against unemployment... (3) Everyone who works has the right to just and favourable remuneration ensuring for himself and his family an existence worthy of human dignity, and supplemented, if necessary, by other means of social protection...

So perhaps we need to look more closely at the robbers in this parable and ask ourselves why people live a life of hate, anger and violence. Their behaviour should not be excused but getting to the root cause will help prevent further crime. As Jesus said of his executioners, 'Father, forgive them; for they do not know what they are doing' (Luke 23:34).

Robbers and thieves, perpetrators of crime – who is guilty and who is the victim? If we examine our incarceration rates, those who are sentenced for crimes are often victims of previous crimes. They are those who have experienced poverty, desperation and violence and, as Richard Rohr observes, 'Much male anger is actually male sadness'.[27]

So in this parable one may well ask, who are the victims? Is it:

The desperate robbers?

The beaten man who was physically abused?

The priest and Levite who must constantly conform to expectations?

The Samaritan who faced continual scrutiny?

We are all one way or another, socially excluded in a world that divides and separates. Yet the parable criticises this division, promoting, rather, a society of equals. Paul, inspired by Jesus' life message, was able to write, 'There is no longer Jew or Greek, there is no longer slave or free, there is no longer male and female; for all of you are one in Christ Jesus' (Galatians 3:28) and again in Romans 2:11, 'For God shows no partiality'. Furthermore, in Paul's Letter to the Romans he writes, 'associate with the lowly' (Romans 12:16), 'live peaceably with all' (Romans 12:18) and he even goes so far as to write, 'if your enemies are hungry, feed them' (Romans 12:20). It is not just the needy, but even those we despise, who must also be the focus of our care and attention, maybe even those robbers. As

---

27 Richard Rohr, *On the Threshold of Transformation. Daily Meditations for Men*, (Chicago: Loyola Press, 2010), Xvii.

Lorraine Hansberry writes in *A Raisin in the Sun:*

> There is always something left to love. And if you ain't learned that, you ain't learned nothing. Have you cried for that boy today? I don't mean for yourself and for the family 'cause we lost the money. I mean for him: what he been through and what it done to him. Child, when do you think is the time to love somebody the most? When they done good and made things easy for everybody? Well, then, you ain't through learning – because that ain't the time at all. It's when he's at his lowest and can't believe in hisself 'cause the world done whipped him so! When you starts measuring somebody, measure him right, child, measure him right. Make sure you done taken into account what hills and valleys he come through before he got to wherever he is.[28]

Why would God insist on care in the most difficult of situations? As Robert W. Funk clearly perceives, 'The Samaritan is not about a stickup on Jericho boulevard at all; it is about a new order of things, a new reality sense, that lies beyond, but just barely beyond, the everyday, the habituated, the humdrum.'[29] The

---

28 Lorraine Hansberry, *A Raisin in the Sun.* Act III, Scene 1, p. 145.
https://khdzamlit.weebly.com/uploads/1/1/2/6/11261956/a_raisin_in_the_sun_-_lorraine hansberry.pdf
29 Robert W. Funk, 'From Parable to Gospel: Domesticating the Tradition,' in *Funk on Parables: Collected Essays* (Santa Rosa,

simple truth is, life is only better when we offer love generously to one another, and when we are recipients of love. We can choose to live in a cold, hard world, each to their own, undisturbed by the pain around us, but what a lonely and miserable 'life' that is. Or we can open ourselves to one another. It is in service, in giving and receiving, that we truly experience 'life'. Mother Teresa encountered Christ 'in distressing disguise'. She was able to see Christ in victims and in perpetrators of crime.

An initiative that has arisen from the teachings of the parable of the Good Samaritan, is Neighbourhood Watch that encourages people is to be concerned for the safety of their neighbourhood. It is based on a number of principles. First, there is communication, knowing who your neighbours are and acknowledging them. Secondly, waving and saying hello can deter an outsider, as well as signifying that you are communicating and watching out for one another. Thirdly, good neighbours also acknowledge those people they do not know, thus letting potential intruders know that they have been seen and observed. This potentially reduces the opportunity for crime to occur.[30]

Those who can be with us in our times of suffering are the ones worthy of being called neighbour and friend. What need do we have of anyone else?

CA: Polebridge, 2006), p. 146.
   30 Get Involved. Neighbourhood Watch. https://www.nhw.wa.gov.au/Get-Involved

The journey begins with trouble on the horizon

... who stripped him...

In reading the parable of the Good Samaritan, do we delve into the character of the beaten man and ask ourselves:

> Who is this man?
> Is he married?
> Does he have a family?
> Is he wealthy?
> Is he well known?
> What nationality?
> What religious affiliation?

The simple answer is, 'We do not know?' and the next response is even more important, 'It does not matter'. Our neighbour can be anyone and should be everyone, no matter their background, culture, faith, no matter their standing in life.

Jesus intentionally leaves the man undescribed. Being in a half dead state he would be unconscious. Since he is stripped, he is unidentifiable. According to Matt Slick, historically, a person can be identified in one of two ways: dress and speech (dialect). The man is any person: void of ethnic background, void of stature and void of position.[31]

The removal of clothes is the stripping of status, nationality, dignity and of all identity. Throughout

---

31 Matt Slick, The Good Samaritan Luke 10:25-37 https://carm.org/parable-good-samaritan

time, there have been so many who were vulnerable, exposed, exploited, demeaned, scandalised, shamed and disgraced. Sadly, there are also many who dare to leer at the nakedness of others.

We hide behind our clothes or believe that the 'clothes make the person', as the saying goes. Not much has changed. Labels matter to us, from the shoes we wear, to the handbags that dangle from our arms. It has to be Oroton or Chanel or Prada, etc. We can spend ridiculous amounts on clothing and accessories as a way to tell others just who we are. Yet who are we really, once these external items are taken away?

We are so enamoured with what we have, our possessions, that we forget what we are made of. Are we made of clothes and glamour, or character and spirit? It just may well be necessary to lose what we have in order to gain who we are.

Life is about letting go of what we believed we needed, our security, our identity, our comfort and our possessions. Life can give and life can take. In the end, we are bare, naked and vulnerable. Yet, when everything is taken from us, we see life as it really is, unshackled, simple and free. When all is laid bare, we are more than what we appeared to be. If we could only enter deeper, we would discover no shame, but inner strength.

The world as we live in it advertises passing fads after passing fads. Nothing endures. It is a stage to display new styles, new pleasures, new technology, new careers, new opportunities, new thrills, new creations and new gadgets. However, they are all illusory, fading and lacking depth. So what if we are promoted, travel to exotic places, move up in the world, own a mansion, or purchase the latest gadget? So what if we are popular, beautiful, tall, successful, rich, eloquent, famous, talented, intelligent, in demand... so what?

So then what does matter? What adds eternal value? What does not fade with the passing of time? And if it does matter, it must speak to one and all. It cannot be of real value if it is exclusive. What is worth pursuing and adds meaning to our lives, not just a shallow passing fad, but an enduring value? What is it? What matters? Naomi Judd provides insight when she writes:

> Every crisis offers a treasure trove of information about ourselves. (That's why they call it an emergency – you emerge and see.) A crisis prompts us to raise our consciousness and choose to open up to more of who we're meant to be. It also shows us just how many more dimensions there are to living. In the Chinese language, the word 'crisis' is made up of two characters, depicting 'danger' and 'opportunity'. It's always up to you and me to choose, at every crossroads, which path we take.[32]

---

[32] Naomi Judd, *Naomi's Breakthrough Guide*, 6 January 2004. https://www.today.com/popculture/naomis-breakthrough-guide-1C9017392

So what is the treasure hidden in the field (Matthew 13:44) and the pearl of great price (Matthew 13:45-46) that matters to us?

... *beat him, and went away, leaving him half dead...*

The robbers beat and robbed the man within an inch of his life. There is deep seated hatred and anger in this single line. The violent nature of people can be terrifying. What gets people to a stage where they physically, mercilessly and repeatedly attack another, be it a stranger or not? Whether the robbers attacked out of desperation or because the person before them was of another race or faith, violence cannot be justified. Rage, anger and hatred arise in us, but if it leads to physical or mental harm of another, it is always wrong. There is never justification for the horrors and injuries committed on another. You choose to do violence or not. You choose to overcome stereotypes or not.

David G. Benner notes that evil is a consequence of choices. No one is born evil. Evil may have roots in personal histories, and the capacity for evil may be inherent in human nature, but what brings evil into existence is the choices made about the way we respond to the things. When wounds are left raw, the only recourse, according to Benner, is to protect our vulnerability by externalising the toxicity that has been internalised. The expression of anger empowers and distances us from the vulnerability of the original emotional wounds. This empowerment can be quite addictive, and expressing it can strengthen rather than lessen the rage.[33]

Yet violent people should not be left to wreak havoc, unaccountable for the devastation they do, the fear they arouse, the harm they enact, the lives they destroy. If we do not work for a better society, if we do not speak out, we give permission for a society of chaos, violence and injustice. Who will call these people to account when we turn a blind eye and walk away?

To hurt, abuse, harm a human being, no matter who they are, or what they have done, is a crime against dignity, the victims as well as the perpetrators. No one wins. All are scarred. Only a greater human act can restore. In times of distress, suffering and injustice, we all need assistance and every person present is called to respond.

We have a great deal of work to do in regards to our inner intentions, our perceptions of others, our attitudes, our preconceived notions, our racism, and our suspicious minds. But we do not do the inner ground work because we do not admit we have anything to address.

So we see a person who has had a bad stroke of luck, who finds themselves knocked to the ground, who

---
[33] David G. Benner, *Human Being and Becoming. Living the Adventure of Life and Love*, (Grand Rapids, Michigan: BrazosPress, 2016), 64.

have fallen to their knees. What is our attitude towards them? Maybe the man deserved to be knocked to the ground because:

> Why was he foolish enough to walk the treacherous road alone?
> He is of a religious faith that is violent and so he gets what he deserves.
> He is of a racial background that are known for their thieving ways.
> He was probably involved in underhanded business and it was payback time.
> You get what you deserve.
> What comes around goes around.

But then if that is the case, it is a dog eat dog world, or as we read in Exodus 21:23-24, 'If any harm follows, then you shall give life for life, eye for eye, tooth for tooth, hand for hand, foot for foot'. This is an endless cycle of tit-for-tat. We have no say, we should not interfere, and each to their own. Violence begets violence, hate perpetuates hate and all we need to do is sidestep the problems and protect me, myself and I. Yet with such an attitude, life becomes an endless cycle of dodging evil and hate. It is survival of the fittest. There is no room for mercy, for compassion, or for God for that matter. Yet Oscar Romero sends a very loud and clear message:

> It would be a shame to have lived so surrounded with the presence of Christ because we are surrounded with the poor and not to have recognised him. To have lived so many years in comfort, with riches, politically well off and not to have been concerned with that Christ who was at our doors or whom we met in the streets.[34]

Jesus was nailed to the cross as a way to oppress him, to control him, to lock him up and so restrict his freedom. And the cross stands firmly against the horizon, a sign of contradiction, nailing anyone who dares challenge current thinking, paralysing them. And many today who look at the crucifix, gaze on the spectacle, bemused, curious or unfazed. Have we become so numb to the pain of others? Are we mere spectators in life?

How are we to learn once again how to notice and empathise with people cast to the wayside, the anonymous and hidden figures? Are people on the margins, hidden from our view, because we want it that way? Do we notice those incapable of getting out of the rut, battered and bruised, body and soul, the homeless, the poor, the abused, the sick, the elderly, the addicted, the lonely, the refugee? Do we stop to see or do we even care? Maybe it is our very selves – lost, broken,

---

[34] Oscar Romero, 26 November 1978; *Daily Meditations*, translated by Irene Hodgson, (St Anthony Press, 2005), 79.

vulnerable, unsure, ridiculed, hurt, confused, hesitant, that needs help.

We were led to believe we were so right, so invincible, so assured. But there comes a time in life when everything crumbles around us, when we give way to hurts and pains. What in us is hurting? Is bound? Is silenced? There are many issues out there that each and every one of us is exposed to:

Stereotyping
Indifference
Substance abuse
Physical violence
Mental health issues
Cyberbullying
Domestic violence
Poverty
War
Unemployment
Suicidal thoughts
Depression
Loneliness
Racism
Ridicule

Where we have played a role in perpetuating these circumstances, it is clearly now time to stop, to cease being the issue, the problem, the perpetrator, or the cause. It is now time to be the merciful, the healer, the humble one, the lover and forgiver.

Maybe in the sorrow and frustration experienced, we may find the courage to truly oppose abuse and violence. We cannot weep forever, but in our experience of suffering and helplessness, a resilience is born and a defiance of corrupt systems grows in the heart. As Richard Rohr notes:

> every biblical hero, at some point on the journey, was forced to leave the worlds of position, privilege, perk, and power, to be able to hear and speak the truth at a deeper level. We can pay a high price for spiritual transformation. Here is where we join Joseph, thrown into the pit by his brothers; Jonah thrown into the belly of the beast by his shipmates; Jeremiah thrown into the muddy cistern by his religious denomination; Job thrown onto the dunghill by his own self-doubt; and Jesus on the cross, carrying the absurdity and evil of the whole lot.[35]

Can we make life a blessing, rather than a heavy burden and stumbling block for others? Do we lift the crosses of others, or do we weigh others down with it? How much have we dared to love? We read in the Gospels, 'Whoever does not carry the cross and follow me cannot be my disciple' (Luke 14:27). For to carry our cross is to:

---

35 Richard Rohr, *On the Threshold of Transformation. Daily Meditations for Men*, (Chicago: Loyola Press, 2010), 184.

Face whatever life confronts us with
Know the weight of sin and suffering
Understand what turmoil is
Experience the injustices and hurts that enter life
Learn endurance and perseverance
Become more merciful towards ourself and others

The cross reminds us that life can be unfair, it can be hard. It reminds us of human hate, human cruelty and human anger. Yet the cross saves us from our own self-importance and self-deception. Only in our difficult experiences can we really know our capacities and inner strengths. It leads us to seek redemption in God's gracious mercy and love. The mystic Julian of Norwich writes in *Revelations of Divine Love*, 'First the fall, and then the recovery from the fall, and both are the mercy of God'.

The traveller in the parable is stripped, beaten and left half dead in a ditch. Luke describes him as having 'wounds', the Greek word being *traumata*, meaning 'trauma'. The man is in a very critical state, like so many other people before and after him. Yet, we have the capacity to heal, to love, to rise above what shames and hurts. It is a life-long practice, learning to accept, learning to let go, learning to believe in ourselves and in God's mercy, despite everything going against us.

Humans are best when they are empowered, standing tall, a strong source for others. Yet in our standing, can we bend over to pull others up? As Jesus says, 'Strive to enter through the narrow door; for many, I tell you, will try to enter and will not be able' (Luke 13:24). Yet the reality is, we do not want to enter the narrow door and be involved. We choose rather to avoid dealing with mess. Yet sometimes we have to do what we would rather not. We have to roll up our sleeves and get into the thick of things and get messy as we extend a helping hand. As Jesus says, 'Not my will, but yours be done' (Luke 22:42). It is our approach to life, hesitant or willing, fearful or courageous, self-serving or serving others, that determines if God's will is done. Will we save another's life, or preserve our own?

The passage in regards to the robbers, and in the next few passages in regards to the passersby, throws a few challenges at us:

Is forgiveness or acts of mercy an occasional act or continual acts on our part?

Is the suffering of others continually playing out because of our selective blindness?

Can we rebuild others with hope, rather than tearing down?

In the Genesis account of Joseph and his brothers, Joseph responds to the suffering inflicted upon him by his brothers by valiantly stating, 'Even though you intended to do harm to me, God intended it for good' (Genesis 50:20). We wonder: can we be so affirmative in our downfall and can we believe good can come out of our present troubles?

Chapter 5

The passersby

Now by chance a priest was going down that road; and when he saw him, he passed by on the other side. So likewise a Levite, when he came to the place and saw him, passed by on the other side.

Luke 10:31-32

Now by chance a priest was going down that road...

The parable places the priest first on the scene for a reason – he was expected to be the one that was likeliest to do something for the victim. The priest would have been considered to be the neighbour. He would be the one a person would look to in their dire need. He would be expected to practise what he preached. The one meant to offer healing balm, prayers, comfort, assurance, assistance and empathy. The priest represented God and God would be expected to right injustice and offer care, as was the message conveyed throughout the Scriptures:

> Hear, O Lord, when I cry aloud, be gracious to me and answer me! (Psalm 27:7)
>
> Hear the voice of my supplication, as I cry to you for help, as I lift up my hands towards your most holy sanctuary. (Psalm 28:2)
>
> Give justice to the weak and the orphan; maintain the right of the lowly and the destitute. Rescue the weak and the needy; deliver them from the hand of the wicked. (Psalm 82:3-4)

How far from this image was the priest. Rather, on approaching the man, 'when he saw him, he passed by on the other side' (v. 31). The priest sees the man in the ditch. It is not just a glance. Literally – in English – he passes beside and over and against.

Yet, there are those who argue in defence of the priest's actions, or lack thereof, because priests were supposed to be ritually clean, exemplars of the law. There would be shame and embarrassment for defilement in making contact with a bleeding person.

> This shall be a perpetual statute for the Israelites and for the alien residing among them. Those who touch the dead body of any human being shall be unclean for seven days. They shall purify themselves with the water on the third day and on the seventh day, and so be clean; but if they do not purify themselves on the third day

and on the seventh day, they will not become clean. All who touch a corpse, the body of a human being who has died, and do not purify themselves, defile the tabernacle of the Lord; such persons shall be cut off from Israel. Since water for cleansing was not dashed on them, they remain unclean; their uncleanness is still on them. (Numbers 19:10-13)

Restoring ritual purity was time-consuming and costly, explains Matt Slick. Moreover, he cannot approach closer than a few metres to a dead man without being defiled, and he will have to overstep that boundary just to ascertain the condition of the wounded man.[36] So how can he be sure the wounded man is a neighbour since he cannot be identified? If the person lying there is a non-Jew the priest could be risking defilement, especially if the person were dead. The law for approaching a corpse was clear in the Scriptures:

> The Lord said to Moses: Speak to the priests, the sons of Aaron, and say to them: No one shall defile himself for a dead person among his relatives, except for his nearest kin: his mother, his father, his son, his daughter, his brother; likewise, for a virgin sister, close to him

---

[36] Matt Slick, The Good Samaritan Luke 10:25-37 https://carm.org/parable-good-samaritan

because she has had no husband, he may defile himself for her. (Leviticus 21:1-3)

They shall not defile themselves by going near to a dead person; for father or mother, however, and for son or daughter, and for brother or unmarried sister they may defile themselves. After he has become clean, they shall count seven days for him. On the day that he goes into the holy place, into the inner court, to minister in the holy place, he shall offer his sin-offering, says the Lord God. (Ezekiel 44:25-27)

If, on the other hand, 'half dead' means that the man is close to death, then the priest must come to the aid of the man. But perhaps the man in the ditch is only a decoy for robbers who will attack the priest when he stops to help. So the priest does the most sensible thing, and rushes on past the beaten man.

Yet Amy-Jill Levine argues against the claim that the priest and the Levite pass by the man in the ditch, because they are afraid of contracting corpse contamination and so violating purity laws. There is nothing impure about touching a person who is 'half dead'. Nor is there any sin involved in burying a corpse; on the contrary, the Torah expected corpses to be interred and the Law required that both men attend to the fellow in the ditch, whether alive or dead, for one is to 'love the neighbour' and 'love the stranger' both.

Neither Jesus nor Luke gives the priest or Levite an excuse. Nor would any excuse be acceptable. Their responsibility was to save a life; they failed. Saving a life is so important that Jewish Law mandates that it override every other concern, including keeping the Sabbath (e.g., 1 Maccabees 2:31–41; 2 Maccabees 6:11; Mishnah, *Shabbat* 18:3). Their responsibility, should the man have died, was to bury the corpse. They failed here as well.[37]

Can we too really justify our failure to act in similar circumstances? Do we allow fear to command our mind over the actions of the heart? Philip Sheldrake writes:

> Spiritualities that are disengaged from the world rather than committed to it, and to its transformation, fail to reflect the irrevocable commitment of God to the world in Jesus Christ.[38]

We are not passersby. God puts people on our path for a reason. Do we sidestep our issues, ignore and turn a blind eye? The statistics today suggest this is the pattern.

---

37 Amy-Jill Levine, *Go and Do Likewise: Lessons from the parable of the Good Samaritan,* 17 September 2014 https://www.americamagazine.org/faith/2014/09/17/go-and-do-likewise-lessons-parable-good-samaritan

38 Philip Sheldrake, *Spirituality and Theology: Christian Living and the Doctrine of God,* (Maryknoll, NY:Orbis Books, 1998), 35.

Almost half a million injured Australians are admitted to hospitals every year, with around 12,000 people dying from their injuries. It was the first responders at the scene that made the biggest difference. Knowing how to stop a critical bleed could also mean the difference between a person dying or not. Yet, the Red Cross notes that fewer than five per cent of people in Australia are trained in first aid, one of the lowest rates in the world.[39]

Failure to stop can have life-saving repercussions. Yet, what prevents us from stopping? The two who do not stop are significant people in their own right – a priest and a Levite – well-to-do people in the society of the time – honoured, respected, and with a sense of self-importance.

It is this false sense of superiority that becomes our own worst enemy. We become so identified with what we do, expectations of our role, the impression people have of us, that we must at all costs keep up appearances, save face and maintain this image, so as not to disappoint and let down others, or so our argument goes. Yet is it really the case? Perhaps it is an excuse so that we avoid doing something that may challenge us.

On the other hand, if we were to place this parable in today's context, there is the fear to stop on a lonely

---

39 SBS NEWS 7/09/2017 Most Australians don't know first aid https://www.sbs.com.au/news/most-australians-don-t-know-first-aid

road if you are a woman walking by. A woman alone on a deserted road may have every desire to stop and assist one in need, but there is the valid fear that they may be targeted and sexually or violently abused. So do we risk our safety? Perhaps the more fundamental question is why is it unsafe to walk alone?

Every incident that comes our way is an opportunity in disguise. God is in the details. In fact, if we learned to stop and see, we would realise God is constantly interfering and blessing our lives, even when we stray off the beaten track! Unfortunately, we tend to ignore the difficult stuff, we sidestep challenges, and in the end we pass by God as well. Our lives become a quick trot heading to nothing important because all the while we focused on ourselves and our security, turning a blind eye to what matters.

If we were to bend down and show compassion and become somewhat vulnerable, who knows what troubles we may tangle ourselves in! So why burden ourselves with untimely issues that are really no concern of ours. Someone else, better qualified, can deal with it. So we walk away or as Michael Tubbs tells the story:

> And then a priest came by, saw the man on the side of the road, maybe said a silent prayer, hopes and prayers, prayers that he gets better. Maybe saw the man on the side of the road and surmised

that it was ordained by God for this particular man, this particular group to be on the side of the road, there's nothing I can do to change it... After the priest walked by, maybe a politician walked by... Saw the man on the side of the road and saw how beat up the man was, saw that the man was a victim of violence, or fleeing violence. Maybe the politician said, "Maybe this man chose to be on the side of the road". That if he just pulled himself up by his bootstraps, despite his boots being stolen, and got himself back on the horse, he could be successful, and there's nothing I could do.[40]

Sometimes we cannot do much, let alone change the world, but we can always do something good, no matter how small it seems, rather than do nothing. To be truly human is to be moved to act with love always, or as the Australian singer Sia and Labrinth put it, 'To be human is to love, even when it gets too much. I'm not ready to give up'.

To do nothing is just as wrong as to do evil. Pleading not guilty, ignorance, or claiming it is not my business, any failure to lend a helping hand, is unpardonable. Jesus made this point clear in Matthew 25:31-46 in his parable of the Judgment of the Nations.

---

[40] Michael Tubbs: The political power of being a good neighbor | TED Talk, April 2019.
https://www.ted.com/talks/michael_tubbs_the_political_power_of_being_a_good_neighbor

When the Son of Man comes in his glory, and all the angels with him, then he will sit on the throne of his glory. All the nations will be gathered before him, and he will separate people one from another as a shepherd separates the sheep from the goats, and he will put the sheep at his right hand and the goats at the left. Then the king will say to those at his right hand, 'Come, you that are blessed by my Father, inherit the kingdom prepared for you from the foundation of the world; for I was hungry and you gave me food, I was thirsty and you gave me something to drink, I was a stranger and you welcomed me, I was naked and you gave me clothing, I was sick and you took care of me, I was in prison and you visited me'. Then the righteous will answer him, 'Lord, when was it that we saw you hungry and gave you food, or thirsty and gave you something to drink? And when was it that we saw you a stranger and welcomed you, or naked and gave you clothing? And when was it that we saw you sick or in prison and visited you?' And the king will answer them, 'Truly I tell you, just as you did it to one of the least of these who are members of my family, you did it to me'. Then he will say to those at his left hand, 'You that are accursed, depart from me into the eternal fire prepared for the devil and his angels; for I was hungry and you gave me no food, I was thirsty and you gave me nothing to drink, I was a stranger and you did not welcome me, naked and you did not give me clothing, sick and in prison and you did not visit me'. Then they also will answer, 'Lord, when was it that we saw you hungry or thirsty or a stranger or naked or sick or in prison, and did not take care of you?' Then he will answer them, 'Truly I tell you, just as you did not do it to one of the least of these, you did not do it to me'. And these will go away into eternal punishment, but the righteous into eternal life.

The parable of the Judgment of the Nations is the one parable that clearly depicts the expectations God has of us. Life has a purpose. We can neither simply give up on life, nor assume life is just about me, myself and I. We live in the world and so we need to be aware of the global context around us, as this forms our very being. Our interactions with everyday events, our relationships with one another, our time, place and culture, all influence us. In the end, we are a product of our time and so we must live fully in the present.

Unfortunately, people create their own little worlds and choose to nestle comfortably there, preferring ignorance and security as their ally. This conflicts with the Gospel teaching to live contributing positively to life, engaged with others. It is about being aware of our surroundings and caring enough to want to do something about it. The hungry, thirsty, stranger, naked, sick, prisoner, anyone destitute, alone, in need, are part of our life. They live in the same world as we do. They breathe the same air and have the same basic needs as we do. So we are one, invited to be one, called to be united.

We are fully human when we are engaged with our sisters and brothers around us. We belong to one another and our responsibility is to care for those who are just like us – vulnerable humans who want and need love.

Referring back to the lawyer's question about eternal life, it is about our deep relationship with God and our neighbour. Unlike the priest and Levite, it is to see others in God's image. It is to be God's image to others, not when it suits, but always; and in the parable of the Good Samaritan it is to be in God's image in circumstances that are most troublesome! As they say, while you are planning your future, life steps in. It is never a neat, straight-forward journey, but one riddled with red lights and road stops.

So when we find ourselves thrown into situations we never imagined, can we be open enough to accept the other without judgment? We could benefit from every person's presence, if we open our hearts. We may be called to do something we do not want to, but it may be our salvation in disguise.

Benjamin Armidale wrote in response to the preparation for the Australian Catholic Plenary Council (2020/21) what he viewed as a necessary change in the Church:

To have the courage to let go the trappings of clericalism. To let go of elitism and exclusion. To embrace the downtrodden, the heart broken, the marginalised. For us to contemplate, how each of us may serve the other? How may we tear down boundaries and take action to walk with others – to show mercy, to forgive, to love. To lead the way in bringing light to darkness – to take action in living-love in all things. To contemplate and act holistically – in our spiritual, social, political, environmental lives.[41]

Sometimes, it is good to be on the other side of the fence, to wear someone else's shoes because then we have the heart to be moved with compassion and to create a better world. We can choose the world we want to live in, and the invitation is to make it a world where we care for one another.

... and when he saw him...

The words 'saw him' are repeated three times in the parable in regards to the priest (v. 31), the Levite (v. 32)

---

[41] Trudy Dantis, Paul Bowell, Stephen Reid and LethDudfield, *Listen to what the Spirit is saying. Final Report for the Plenary Council. Phase 1: Listening and Dialogue,*' (National Centre for Pastoral Research, Australian Catholic Bishops Conference, 2019), 285.
https://plenarycouncil.catholic.org.au/wp content/uploads/2019/09/FINAL-BOOK-v7-online-version-LISTEN-TO-WHAT-THE-SPIRIT-IS-SAYING.pdf

and the Samaritan (v. 33). It is not that the three were not fully aware of the predicament. Each saw and knew. The dilemma was right before their very eyes. However, how they responded to the situation differed.

To see automatically means you are involved in the situation. You become a witness to the scene as we know from watching crime thrillers or read about in police investigations. People at the crime scene must give evidence in court whether they were involved or not. You were there, you saw, so you are part of the investigation. You possess vital information in the unravelling of the mystery.

So we become reluctant participants in the events of life. What we see becomes part of our lives and has an impact. How many have seen a horrific incident and it haunts them throughout their lives? One picture can tell a thousand words. What then would the scene of a terribly beaten man evoke in our minds? Who is not to say that the priest and Levite who walked away were probably traumatised by the scene? Perhaps or perhaps not, but surely that image remained with them for some length of the journey. An image that screamed for help and they were unable to offer any.

Too many times we are paralysed by fear, plagued by doubts, tormented by our incapacities to be able to break free and attend to the needs of others. And we hide the image away with our regrets. And we begin to wonder whether the one who was really in need was ourselves with our inability to do what was life-giving.

There may be chances or coincidences on our life's path but really it is a matter of how we look at the incidences. The priest saw the victim as a problem but in actual fact he should have viewed it as 'by chance'. Mechthild of Magdeburg notes, 'The day of my spiritual awakening was the day I saw and knew I saw all things in God and God in all things'. So how do we see? And what do we see?

We all have our own burdens to carry but are we willing to take on another's burdens in a world where we are prone to dismiss our burdens and claim each to their own? Yet Jesus was ever present to the needs of others and such an example is when he was looking down on Jerusalem and weeping over it.

> 'Jerusalem, Jerusalem, the city that kills the prophets and stones those who are sent to it! How often have I desired to gather your children together as a hen gathers her brood under her wings, and you were not willing!' (Luke 13:34).

The bigger problem, Richard Rohr notes, is that we do not join with Jesus in weeping over history, humanity, and what we have done to one another and the universal 'city' that he stares at.[42]

---

42 Richard Rohr, *On the Threshold of Transformation. Daily Meditations for Men*, (Chicago: Loyola Press, 2010), 242.

When we find ourselves hurled into a situation that is not ours to be involved in, how do we enter it? Do we tag along with what is clearly a wrong event, or do we keep silent, saying it is not for me to interfere, it is not my concern? Or can we see it as 'by chance,' a blessing in disguise?

We fall for the propaganda of self-worship and comfortably extol this contrived value because it inflates our egos and make us self-satisfied and comfortable. That is why we can justify turning a blind eye, averting our gaze, withholding our assistance and walking away. We are people of our time and context who self-worship, a society where it is justified to avoid certain people and circumstances because it is not within our means, agenda, time, finances or responsibility. There are others to do this or that. So who am I to overstep the mark! I am simply paving the way for relevant and more appropriately qualified people to do their part.

Then again, perhaps, if others were around on that road, we might have attended to the man's needs; we would not want to be seen as negligent! Thus, our motives for helping others may not always be sincere. So, do we do a good deed for recognition, or out of concern for another?

On the road, at times we may find ourselves the only ones, and if we fail to stop or do our part, we play a role in continuing to perpetuate that cycle of violence and hatred. Each of us will have our time to intervene, but do we have the courage, or the will power, to step up and step out? Or do we continue on our merry way, oblivious to the tragedies of life that need time, care and healing, that need us to stop, take notice and lend a stretched out hand. It takes boldness, courage and risk.

When we have to do something, we cannot excuse ourselves through fear or self-preservation. Those impossible or difficult situations we encounter are not impossible or difficult if we invite God into the picture. God will accompany us, grace us, and empower us. We have recourse to God, wherever we may find ourselves.

In our journey, we come across people of all walks of life, all are in God's image, if we really open our eyes to see. As Thomas Merton writes in *Conjectures of a Guilty Bystander*:

> In Louisville, at the corner of Fourth and Walnut, in the center of the shopping district, I was suddenly overwhelmed with the realization that I loved all these people, that they were mine and I theirs, that we could not be alien to one another even though we were total strangers. It was like waking from a dream of separateness, of spurious self-isolation in a special world...
> I have the immense joy of being man, a member of a race in which God Himself became incarnate. As if the sorrows and stupidities of the human

condition could overwhelm me, now that I realize what we all are. And if only everybody could realize this! But it cannot be explained. There is no way of telling people that they are all walking around shining like the sun.
Then it was as if I suddenly saw the secret beauty of their hearts, the depths of their hearts where neither sin nor desire nor self-knowledge can reach, the core of their reality, the person that each one is in God's eyes. If only they could all see themselves as they really are. If only we could see each other that way all the time. There would be no more war, no more hatred, no more cruelty, no more greed... But this cannot be seen, only believed and 'understood' by a peculiar gift.[43]

The priest and Levite sidestepped, turned a blind eye, passed by, maybe because it was just easier that way. See no evil, hear no evil, speak no evil. But God is all seeing and all knowing. We can neither escape God, nor run away or hide from others.

The priest and Levite nether stop to assess the situation of the beaten man, nor of the robbers, nor of themselves. Until we stop and take a good look at where we are, we will not see the real truth about ourselves and even less so about others.

---

43 Thomas Merton, *Conjectures of a Guilty Bystander,* (New York: Bantam Doubleday Dell Publishing, 1994), 153-154.

... he passed by on the other side...

The storyteller provides no reason for the priest's action. He just acts that way. This is just the way priests are. At any rate, the storyteller is uninterested in the priest's motives and simply describes his actions. Since Levites were employed in regular temple service, we could rehearse the same set of excuses, argues Bernard Brandon Scott. These two members of the religious elite simply pass by on the other side.[44] Yet no excuse, not our busyness, self-importance, disgust, fear or lack of time will satisfy.

Yet, all too often, we run away instead of speaking out. We are fickle. We are weak. We are manipulated. We make wrong choices. We fear. We fail. We betray. We deny. We fall asleep. We panic. We hide. And because we fail to act, the innocent are victimised, denied justice and face death.

The priest and Levite ignored their invitation to extend a helping hand and the story makes it clear their choice was not the right one. A person of God would be expected to stop and help. We cannot be part time people of faith. We are not into the New Age Spirituality of only picking and choosing what appeals to our sensitivities and so remain satisfied at such a

---

[44] Bernard Brandon Scott, *Re-Imagine the World. An Introduction to the Parables of Jesus*, (California: Polebridge Press, 2010), 60.

superficial level. Religion will make demands on us and challenge us.

In today's world, we are encouraged to leave behind our troubles, let go of what is too difficult, or simply abandon what we do not want to endure. So it sounds archaic, out-of-touch, irrelevant and outdated to say 'carry your cross and bear one another's burdens'. Why should we? It is better to rid ourselves from all that hampers and causes suffering, distance ourselves from that which causes unnecessary grief and pain, because they hinder our human flourishing. That may sound like good advice but there are things in life we cannot run away from, crosses that cannot be ignored. Capacity for resilience does not come from simplifying one's life and avoiding difficulties. It comes from bearing burdens, carrying crosses and growing from struggles. We cannot simply be onlookers, passersby, in the drama of life.

On the road of life, the invitation is truly to let our hearts rule and allow the situation to transform us. There is much to embrace on our journey:

>   Love that is willing to die for another
>   Truth deeper than the mind can fathom
>   Offering of compassion with all its tenderness
>   Forgiveness that does not count the cost
>   The beauty of creation in all its natural splendour
>   The memories of relationships that have
>   journeyed through thick and thin

The passersby

> The sincere person whose words are balm to our aching souls
> The one who holds us in their prayers
> Hope that refuses to fade
> Courage in the face of overwhelming opposition

What matters is to be truly and deeply human to one another. To fall from our pride and begin to notice the little things around us that really are important. To choose to befriend, to smile and welcome, to sit in silence and listen, to lead others to their inner truth, to know God as ever present love. To be love. To be God to one another.

On our road there will be surprises, unanticipated stops and even roundabouts and U-turns, where we need to veer off our road and turn back. Maybe our direction or destination was heading us elsewhere when we really needed to be here. Yes, on our journey life will interrupt us and cause us to divert our attention to what is at hand, but that one stop can make all the difference.

Be careful because the very thing you prefer to avoid on your journey, the very thing you fear or disdain, may very well be the one thing that is your salvation. Blessings come in disguises. The ugly can be the beautiful. The painful can be the means to growth. The person in need may be the very one to awaken us to a deeper purpose in our comings and goings.

There is a story told about Francis of Assisi who in his younger years was a rich and pampered young man. One night, he set off on his horse for a night of drinking and pleasure. Riding down a narrow road, he found his path blocked by a leper whose deformity and smell of rotting flesh revolted him. Francis was unable to steer his horse around the leper. He had no choice but to get down off his horse and move the leper out of his path. As he put out his hand and touched the leper's arm, suddenly, irrationally and unashamed, he kissed the leper. In that kiss, Francis found the reality of God and of love in a way that would change his life forever.

We are meant to come down from our high horse and stretch out our hand and to overstep the mark, to push boundaries, break rules and taboos, and to come to our own decisions, arriving at a new enlightenment. Otherwise, we remain stuck in our old ways, making the same assumptions over and over again. We become compliant, passive, non-threatening, in a world that wants to tame, blind and silence us to the wrongs of the world.

Sometimes, the patterns of our daily life need to be challenged, questioned, debated, rewritten and more so when they refrain us from doing what must be done.

An oft quoted study is that of John M. Darley and C. Daniel Batson, who used the Good Samaritan as their starting point:

> People going between two buildings encountered a shabbily dressed person slumped by the side of the road. Subjects in a hurry to reach their destination were more likely to pass by without stopping. Some subjects were going to give a short talk on the parable of the Good Samaritan, others on a nonhelping relevant topic; this made no significant difference in the likelihood of their giving the victim help. Religious personality variables did not predict whether an individual would help the victim or not. However, if a subject did stop to offer help, the character of the helping response was related to his type of religiosity.[45]

They then concluded:

> The frequently cited explanation that ethics becomes a luxury as the speed of our daily lives increases is at least an accurate description... According to the reflections of some of the subjects, it would be inaccurate to say that they

---

[45] John M. Darley and C. Daniel Batson, 'From Jerusalem To Jericho': A Study Of Situational And Dispositional Variables In Helping Behavior in *Journal of Personality and Social Psychology* 1973, Vol. 27, No. J, 100. https://greatergood.berkeley.edu/images/uploads/Darley-JersualemJericho.pdf

realized the victim's possible distress, then chose to ignore it; instead, because of the time pressures, they did not perceive the scene in the alley as an occasion for an ethical decision. For other subjects it seems more accurate to conclude that they decided not to stop. They appeared aroused and anxious after the encounter in the alley... And this is often true of people in a hurry; they hurry because somebody depends on their being somewhere. Conflict, rather than callousness, can explain their failure to stop. Finally... considerable variations were possible in the kinds of help given, and these variations did relate to personality measures – specifically to religiosity of the quest sort... whether a person helps or not is an instant decision likely to be situationally controlled. How a person helps involves a more complex and considered number of decisions, including the time and scope to permit personality characteristics to shape them.[46]

So being the Good Samaritan tends to depend on a person's time, workload, pre-occupation and other factors, along with their religiosity.

Considering the study by Darley and Batson, what are the avoidance mechanisms we perhaps unconsciously put into place to 'pass by' issues today?

---

46 Darley, 'From Jerusalem To Jericho': A Study Of Situational And Dispositional Variables In Helping Behavior, 107-108.

The passersby

> We avert our gaze from what frightens us
> Selective hearing, omitting the groans of those in pain
> Excuses and matters of urgency clamour our priorities
> Workaholic to avoid reality
> Detours to avoid certain encounters
> Claiming incompetence and ignorance
> Siding with stereotypes, racism, scapegoating, etc.

How often are we of assistance to another? Is it the pattern that we see in the parable, that only once in every three occasions, we show some sort of care? I would venture to say that is more generous than what is in reality our true behaviour. All too often, our compassionate attention tends to take a backseat. We hurry along. We do not choose to stop. The offering of our service and mercy has been undervalued to the detriment of both the one in need and ourselves. If we do not stop to build up the other, what then are we building up?

And if we pass by God in the first beaten person, will we do so when we encounter the next person, or the following person? When will we stop and encounter God in our fallen sisters and brothers?

So many things pass us by because we have lacked engagement. Our attitude is one of *laissez faire*. Opportunities come and go and we remain as we are.

We do not commit to life fully. We do not grasp life with a passion. We pass by without noticing the life around us and life passes us by while we sit and wallow in our own small self-interests.

Today, there is a growing trend of indifference or apathy. We are so removed from reality. We have cocooned ourselves in our little worlds and avoid anything that may awaken us to the lie we are living. We coddle ourselves in luxuries, cars, labels or health regimes. We want to get and do whatever we want. Why should we have to worry, compromise, give in to, all for someone else? We have become a generation of so called independent people, who are oblivious to the fact that everything around us was because of other people and that we are dependent on others to ensure our needs are met.

Apathy, disinterest, nonchalant attitudes – these are what the priest and Levite display. It may be a harsh call, but the fact is they left a dying man on the road, without batting an eyelid. Yes apathy is the greatest sin. Fear is a close second when it paralyses us from undertaking the right actions.

The solution to apathy is to learn to immerse ourselves in experience, in daily life, to mingle with everyone and not consider ourselves better than others, but rather equals. Not to give ear to ideas and thoughts that criticise others and that devalue the human. To listen to the heart, stretch out a helping hand so that it becomes a habit.

The destination matters but it is the journey that determines our ultimate destination. We can no longer be of the priest and Levite style – distant, aloof, judgmental and self-serving. A movement towards a Samaritan model is needed – humble, attentive, compassionate, healing, service, gentle, present and understanding.

People have been hurt in some way or other. They need a very different place to turn to, a place where they need not live in fear and pain. A 'heaven on earth', rather, than as the lawyer insisted, seeking eternal life. Here and now must become a place of comfort, healing, hope and joy.

God is here, each and every time we come across another. Day by day, God is here, before us. Day by day, we are called to be like God to one another. To care for one another day by day, moment by moment.

We have become so far removed from the reality of this world of pain that we urgently need to return to a heart of flesh. We cannot be a church, Christians, a people of dry bones, that rattle loudly but have no purpose. As Ezekiel writes in 37:1-6,

> The hand of the Lord came upon me, and he brought me out by the spirit of the Lord and set me down in the middle of a valley; it was full

of bones. He led me all round them; there were very many lying in the valley, and they were very dry. He said to me, 'Mortal, can these bones live?' I answered, 'O Lord God, you know'. Then he said to me, 'Prophesy to these bones, and say to them: O dry bones, hear the word of the Lord. Thus says the Lord God to these bones: I will cause breath to enter you, and you shall live. I will lay sinews on you, and will cause flesh to come upon you, and cover you with skin, and put breath in you, and you shall live; and you shall know that I am the Lord'.

We are called to be a Church, Christians, people of flesh, not of bones. We are called to action. To enflesh love. Jesus said in Luke 5:31, 'Those who are well have no need of a physician, but those who are sick'. We lead by example. What we do has repercussions for others. Our actions reap their own rewards. If we stop to help another, we will find mercy is shown to us.

Putting people before our own concerns and agendas is an art of living we need to relearn. Otherwise we fail the art of living. We become humans too busy being human doings, rather than truly being human beings.

So likewise a Levite, when he came to the place and saw him, passed by on the other side.

The Levite followed the priest; he imitated his actions. The Levite abandons the beaten man just as the priest did. It is the crowd mentality. We justify our actions because the majority did the same thing before us. The odds are with us so there must be some right in what we do. We learn our behaviours from what we see others do and then take comfort in knowing everyone else follows suit. We do not have to use our discernment.

The Levite is the routine person, the dutiful one who does what they are told and never steps out of line. The masses who are drilled in ways and practices that they have forgotten how to think for themselves and feel for others. They simply follow the law and imitate the person before them. They do not want to be the one to make change, to think outside the square, to take initiative in doing something new and perhaps challenging. The compliant ones, who think they are doing the right thing and want to avoid any trouble. Yet in their own obedient ways, whose respect have they really earned and whose respect have they foregone? Neil Brown correctly perceived:

> A mechanical application of general rules, therefore, is both an abdication of responsibility and a practice which is potentially dangerous

to those affected by it, because it is prone to misrepresent their real needs and feelings. Each moral judgment should be a sensitive determination of where the true good lies in these particular circumstances. It is there that the voices of victims of new injustices may be heard, where new sensitivities have the opportunity to emerge, and where faith is allowed to call us prophetically to new levels of compassion and service. Without such renewal, a moral system becomes itself a form of oppression. The final test of the relationship of our faith to our moral life can only be, therefore, its effectiveness in keeping our minds and hearts open to the real needs of our neighbour and of ourselves.[47]

Why should we do something different, why buck the trend, when it is easier to leave good enough alone? And anyway those who are 'better' than us, the more knowledgeable ones on these matters – in this case the priest – set the trend, so we cannot be blamed if what we did was wrong.

There is always safety in numbers, so why stand out, or go against the flow, or rock the boat? It will only get you entangled in issues and your reward is just more of a headache. Let it be as it is. God will take care of the situation and someone else will do it.

---

[47] Neil Brown, 'Uniting Faith and the Moral Life' in *An Introduction to Catholic Theology*, edited by Richard Lennan, (New Jersey: Paulist Press, 1998), 160.

The passersby

Yet it is you and I who are meant to bring people back into health, into acceptance and into the fold, not someone else. It is up to us to walk with the wounded. The priest and Levite needed to listen to their hearts. We all come to a point in life where we have to question ourselves and admit that our inner conflict is telling us something is not right here. There comes a time when we feel the need to help others less fortunate, or do we...

A recent study was undertaken by Ted Bergstrom.[48] In the scenario, you are driving along a lonely road, and come upon a stalled car and a motorist who appears to have run out of petrol. You consider stopping to offer help, although this may cost you several minutes and some extra driving. Would your decision be different if the road were more heavily travelled? Bergstrom concluded:

> Each player would take a socially beneficial action if she knew that no one else would do it, but in the symmetric equilibrium, when players account for the probability that somebody else will do it, the probability that nobody takes action increases with group size... When costs of stopping differ among individuals, we find

---

48 Ted Bergstrom, 'The Good Samaritan and Traffic on the Road to Jericho' in *American Economic Journal: Microeconomics* 2017, 9(2): 33–53 (pp49-50) https://doi.org/10.1257/mic.20150296 33
https://pubs.aeaweb.org/doi/pdfplus/10.1257/mic.20150296

that, although individuals are less likely to help where traffic is more dense, a stranded traveller faces a shorter expected waiting time for help to arrive because potential helpers arrive more frequently.

While our fable of a traveller in distress, taken literally, may seem to have narrow application, I believe that it offers insight into a large number of similar situations where people encounter an unsatisfactory state of affairs and must decide whether to fix the problem or leave it for someone who will encounter it later.

Bergstrom proposes, 'Perhaps the priest and the Levite who hurried past the injured traveller had good excuses. Maybe they had important things to do and realised that if they did not stop, someone less busy would soon be likely to appear and perform the rescue'. Yet Jeff Bloem argues that perhaps the priest and the Levite thought someone else would come along on the (busy) road to Jericho and help the injured traveller, but they would have never expected that a Samaritan would stop, and that is the main point of the parable.[49]

All of us harbour within us implicit bias, the unconscious attitude or stereotypes that affect our

---

[49] Jeff Bloem, *An Economist Takes on the Parable of the Good Samaritan*, April 27, 2017
https://jeffbloem.wordpress.com/2017/04/27/an-economist-takes-on-the-parable-of-the-good-samaritan/

decisions and actions. Implicit bias unconsciously affects how we think, feel and act towards others, based on race, ethnicity or appearance.[50] The priest and Levite displayed explicit bias which included prejudice evident in their opinions and actions. However, they also carried implicit bias which is unconscious, involuntary and unintentional. It is the result of subconscious associations the brain makes, based on experiences one has had starting at a very young age.[51] Yet whatever bias we have, ultimately we are meant to overcome them. As Haim G. Ginott, notes:

> I have come to the frightening conclusion that I am the decisive element. It is my personal approach that creates the climate. It is my daily mood that makes the weather. I possess tremendous power to make life miserable or joyous. I can be a tool of torture or an instrument of inspiration, I can humiliate or honour, hurt or heal. In all situations, it is my response that decides whether a crisis is escalated or de-escalated, and a person is humanized or de-humanized. If we treat people as they are, we make them worse. If we treat people as they ought to be, we help them become what they are capable of becoming.[52]

---

50 J. Paul Nyquist, *Is Justice Possible? The elusive pursuit of what is right*, (Chicago: Moody Publishers, 2017), 76.
51 Nyquist, 77.
52 Haim G. Ginott, *Teacher and Child: A Book for Parents and Teachers*, (United Kingdom: Prentice Hall, 1993), 5.

A GoFundMe page was set up to assist Australian Survivor contestant Luke Toki who was eliminated despite the fact that his two boys were both on the autism spectrum and his baby daughter Madeline, born just six weeks before *Survivor* started filming, has cystic fibrosis. Throughout the season, he was vocal about his intentions, 'to take out the title of Sole Survivor and, in turn, win $500k to provide a better life for them'.[53] The initial GoFundMe target of $500,000 was reached within hours and is an example of the fact that humans do care and are moved by those less fortunate or hard done by, contrary to the priest and Levite actions.

Again in late 2019 and early 2020, Australia experienced destructive fires never seen before. Not only did many Australians rally behind the victims of the fires but there was an international effort. Firefighters came from the United States and Canada. New Zealand, Singapore and Papua New Guinea offered military support. French President Emmanuel Macron called Prime Minister Scott Morrison to offer operational assistance and support, joining world leaders including the British royal family. International celebrities have also donated generously to Australian bushfire victims.[54]

---

53 Survivor Australia: GoFundMe for Luke surpasses Pia's prize money https://www.news.com.au/entertainment/tv/reality-tv/australian-survivor/survivors-luke-toki-on-track-to-surpass-winning-prize-with-viral-gofundme/news-story/af119d0df2ac6175837e45f95f78aa11

54 Nick Bonyhady, 'Call for help': International response to

Then again we had the Covid-19 Pandemic. We were told to be in lockdown and to self-isolate in order to protect ourselves from the virus. But shouldn't we be there, at the side of those afflicted? Our First Aid message DR ABCD has its first message as D – Danger. It convinces us that the first thing is to assess any danger to ourselves. So being in lockdown and self-isolating is for the better good of all. Yet in the situation where you are faced with the decision of what to do, you need to do what should be done. Keep in mind that the Samaritan did not deliberately run up to the beaten man on the road. He just happened to come across him and then he did what should be done. We too were not asked to run out and attend to every person in need during Covid-19 or in other circumstances. However, when we are faced with such circumstances, we are expected to do what we can. And we generally do. In fact we have many people assisting others with acts of kindness.[55]

These three examples suggest humanity can and does care for those down on their luck.

Why are there people who do choose a life of service to others? There are many who desire to be

---

Australian fires,' in *Sydney Morning Herald*, January 6, 2020.
https://www.smh.com.au/politics/federal/call-for-help-international-response-to-australian-fires-20200106-p53p5r.html

55 Luke Michael, The acts of kindness shining through as coronavirus panic takes hold, 20 March 2020.
https://probonoaustralia.com.au/news/2020/03/the-acts-of-kindness-shining-through-as-coronavirus-panic-takes-hold/

nurses, doctors, teachers, psychologists, palliative care workers and so on. There is within the human the need to alleviate pain and assist others, when and where we can. Then there are others, priest and Levite included, who lacked the empathy to feel for the other. It had nothing to do with being obedient to religious or State laws. It was, rather, about lacking capacity to show outreach. To serve another and willingly be by their side is an act of virtue we need to cultivate throughout our lives.

There are many lessons we can learn from the failures of the priest and Levite. We should not pass judgment but allow our hearts to be moved to speak. When we ignore the wounded, we are actually wounded by the absence of the wounded. Therefore, it is wise to step out of routine and be moved with mercy. We cannot live with the paralysing terror of doing the wrong thing, that in the end we do nothing. We need to sit in the weakness of others and of ourself in order to see the strength and truth. When our hearts change so do our structures and it makes room for a more compassionate world.

The priest and Levite, those who do nothing, who fail to act, are painted in sweeping brush strokes. The focus and detail in this parable is on the one who acts, the Samaritan. It is not about our failures. These do not deserve our attention and focus. It is the positive behaviour that merits notice.

Chapter 6

Stopping on the journey

> *But a Samaritan while travelling came near him; and when he saw him, he was moved with pity.*
>
> Luke 10:33

But a Samaritan...

When the Northern Kingdom was captured by the Assyrians in 722 BCE, the Jews intermarried with them to settle in Samaria, north of Judea. Samaritans were ethnic and religious outcasts to many first-century Jews because they were known as half-breeds, half Jewish and half Gentile. Samaria was a cultural and religious potpourri, mixing local pagan customs and cultic mores with the foundational Mosaic tenets, to the point of abandoning the sacred and ancient traditions of Yahweh's people. So Samaritans were viewed by the Jews as worshipping pagan gods and falling into idolatry.

Samaritans only regarded the five books of the Torah as 'Scripture', and had their own version of these texts called the Samaritan Pentateuch. Yet the Samaritans were not gentiles. They were bound by the same laws as the Jews.

> He shall not go where there is a dead body; he shall not defile himself even for his father or mother (Leviticus 21:11)

Samaritans hated the Jews as much as the Jews hated the Samaritans. No insult was greater for the faithful Jew than being called 'a Samaritan' and any traveller through Palestine in Jesus' time would carefully avoid setting foot in Samaria, lest they became morally defiled.

Yet Jesus himself stopped in Samaria. In John chapter 4, we read how it was hot and Jesus was tired and thirsty as he sits alone in the noonday heat. When a Samaritan woman approaches, it is to her that Jesus asks for water. Perhaps his experience with the woman led to him telling the parable of the Good Samaritan, where someone on a lonely road encounters a Samaritan who attends to their needs.

Jesus mentioned the Samaritan in this parable because he would be the least likely to help a Jew. The expected triad is priest, Levite and Israelite. Yet Jesus chooses a shock tactic: priest, Levite and Samaritan!

The use of the Samaritan subverts the conventional perception among ancient Jews that eternal life is the exclusive privilege of their own religious or ethnic community, as detailed in Deuteronomy 7:6, 'For you are a people holy to the Lord your God; the Lord your God has chosen you out of all the peoples on earth to be his people, his treasured possession'. Furthermore, to call the Samaritan in the story 'good' (a word never used in the text) is to participate in a racist assumption that being 'good' is an unusual and noteworthy achievement for Samaritans.[56]

The Samaritan would not be from that area, so the half dead man would certainly not qualify as his neighbour. The Samaritan risks defilement and approaches this unidentifiable man and helps him. In this parable, the one who inherits eternal life because of his love for the needy man is the religious-ethnic outsider and enemy, the Samaritan, the one who refused to leave a fellow human, dying by the roadside.

As well, there is the tacit claim that the priest and Levite would *not* inherit eternal life due to their failure to love the man in need.[57] Not only is the conventional

---

56 Matthew S. Rindge, *Good Samaritan (Luke 10:25-37)*, n.p. [cited 5 June 2019].
https://www.bibleodyssey.org:443/en/passages/main-articles/good-samaritan
57 Matthew S. Rindge, *Good Samaritan (Luke 10:25-37)*, n.p. [cited 5 June 2019].
https://www.bibleodyssey.org:443/en/passages/main-articles/good-samaritan

perception of who inherits eternal life overturned, but so is the perception of who is neighbour and what it means to be a neighbour.

John Dickson states, 'Jesus expected his followers to care for people in need, regardless of race, religion or morality. And by making the Samaritan – not the priest – the hero of this story, he was pointing out that sometimes religion gets in the way of universal compassion'.[58]

... while travelling came near him...

Nothing actually really moves in this parable until the Samaritan comes by and stops! Prior to this, the parable seems stuck in a rut, going nowhere.

- The man comes on to the scene and is immediately beaten and remains where he is for quite some time, unmoving.
- A priest and Levite make a brief appearance but remain 'unmoved' by the plight of the beaten man, who thus remains 'unmoved'.
- However, when a Samaritan comes along, he is 'moved with pity' and from there we have a rapid onset of movements.

---

58 The Good Samaritan - Centre for Public Christianity https://www.publicchristianity.org/the-good-samaritan/

There is movement towards the beaten man
The movement from danger to safety
The movement to the inn
The movement of the Samaritan as he continues on

To put it in a nutshell, unless our hearts are moved, nothing really happens. Change is not instigated, transformation is halted and we are all treading the same cycle.

It is important to note the difference in the way the three characters approach the beaten man:

- a priest was going down that road; and when he saw him, he passed by on the other side.
- a Levite, when he came to the place and saw him, passed by on the other side.
- a Samaritan while travelling came near him; and when he saw him 'He was moved with pity'.

The priest is travelling and then sees. We do not know how close he got but it suggests he was far enough to decide to change gears!

The Levite 'came to the place and saw', so he seems to have been in closer proximity to the beaten man than the priest had come, but the Levite also crosses to the other side.

Whereas a Samaritan comes near first and then he sees. It appears the Samaritan had not deliberately decided to approach closer to inspect the situation. He just happened to stumble upon the beaten man, 'while travelling came near him; and when he saw him, he was moved with pity' (v. 33). The order of what is happening here is important. The Samaritan came close and then saw the beaten man on the road and took pity. It just so happened he basically stumbled upon the man and, being so close to him, he could see firsthand the staggering nature of the injuries and thus naturally took pity. Perhaps if the Samaritan had first seen the man lying on the road from a distance, like the priest seems to have observed, he might well have pretended not to notice and possibly would have hurried on. This may lessen the honour of the Samaritan but what follows matters much more.

Whatever the reason there is in regards to the Samaritan's proximity to the unknown figure lying beaten on a deserted road, the Samaritan decided to assist the beaten man. The reason does not matter. What matters is that he did do something. Isaiah 53:3 is a reminder not to hide our faces from that which screams at us:

> He was despised and rejected by others; a man of suffering and acquainted with infirmity; and as one from whom others hide their faces he was despised, and we held him of no account.

There is the saying 'Out of sight, out of mind'. The quicker people remove themselves from a difficult situation, the quicker they forget about it. We sometimes need to be shoved up close and personal, face to face, before we can acknowledge or feel the pain of the other. This is why restorative justice and juvenile correction are applied as ways in which perpetrators come face to face with their victims, in order to feel their grief and show some remorse.

We hide the difficult things from our view so that we do not have to feel a sense of responsibility towards the other. How close do we have to get to another before we can honestly care for them? How bad must their situation become before we can make an effort to attend to their needs?

Returning back to the passage, the Samaritan arrives at the scene. This is the first point of focus. He comes near. He dares to approach. Fear does not get the better of him. To quote Mary Webb, 'If you stop to be kind, you must swerve often from your path'. Here there is no avoidance of the situation, where generally human nature avoids predicaments.

On our road called life, there are ways to get about. We can go slowly, leisurely, or at breakneck speed. We can travel alone, or with company. We can stop to smell the roses or we can be in a hurry. Then there are times we need a bit of prodding to move along, a bit of encouragement.

The Samaritan went to the victim. To go to another, to narrow the distance, to approach, to come, to be present, to be there. James Martin writes:

> When I lifted the host, I realised that Jesus took his body to so many places; he gave his body to people, physically. He brought himself to people – saying, in essence, 'This is my body. Here I am'.[59]

Jesus stopped a great deal on his road trips to help others in need as we read throughout the Gospels.

> *A leper came to him* begging him, and kneeling he said to him, 'If you choose, you can make me clean'. Moved with pity, Jesus stretched out his hand and touched him, and said to him, 'I do choose. Be made clean!' (Mark 1:40-41)

> *As soon as they left the synagogue, they entered* the house of Simon and Andrew, with James and John. Now Simon's mother-in-law was in bed with a fever, and they told him about her at once. He came and took her by the hand and lifted her up. Then the fever left her, and she began to serve them. (Mark 1:29-31)

---

59 James Martin, *Jesus. A Pilgrimage.* (New York: HarperOne, 2014), 343.

Soon afterwards *he went to a town* called Nain, and his disciples and a large crowd went with him. *As he approached* the gate of the town, a man who had died was being carried out. He was his mother's only son, and she was a widow; and with her was a large crowd from the town. When the Lord saw her, he had compassion for her and said to her, 'Do not weep'. Then he came forward and touched the bier, and the bearers stood still. And he said, 'Young man, I say to you, rise!' The dead man sat up and began to speak, and Jesus gave him to his mother. (Luke 7:11-15)

Then *people came out* to see what had happened, and when they came to Jesus, they found the man from whom the demons had gone sitting at the feet of Jesus, clothed and in his right mind. And they were afraid. (Luke 8:35)

They brought to him a deaf man who had an impediment in his speech; and they begged him to lay his hand on him. *He took him aside* in private, away from the crowd, and put his fingers into his ears, and he spat and touched his tongue. Then looking up to heaven, he sighed and said to him, 'Ephphatha', that is, 'Be opened'. (Mark 7:32-34)

They came to Bethsaida. Some people brought a blind man to him and begged him to touch him. *He took the blind man by the hand and led him out* of the village; and when he had put saliva on his eyes and laid his hands on him, he asked him, 'Can you see anything?' And the man looked up and said, 'I can see people, but they look like trees, walking'. Then Jesus laid his hands on his eyes again; and he looked intently and his sight was restored, and he saw everything clearly. (Mark 8:22-25)

Jesus is the God that comes to us in our darkest moments. When no one else cares, God does. When others avert their gaze, God looks. God does not abandon. God is wherever we may be and however we may be. A God who knows our needs and makes sure we are attended to. A God of love always. A God always near. A God we need.

The ability to feel for another takes us out of ourselves and draws us closer to consider another's circumstances and to do something about it. It is about putting others before ourselves. Peter Varengo instinctively writes:

> Every journey has its encounters, but every journey has crossroads as well, moments and events that not only demand choices and decisions but also will eventually determine the success or failure of the whole journey.[60]

---

[60] Peter Varengo, *We want to see Jesus. Discipleship as a journey of search and commitment,* (Victoria: Coventry Press, 2018), 27.

So people are placed on our path for a purpose. Stop and get to know your companions on the journey. Some could do with assistance, company, a helping hand and a warm presence.

... and when he saw him...

The second point of focus is that the Samaritan sees. To see the other is to take notice, to acknowledge their presence and to come to understanding.

How do we see?

Do we recognise the reality before us?

Do we avoid seeing?

Do we see only what we want to see?

We are called to see not only with our eyes, but with our heart. In a world of speed, to stop and know, as the Psalmist wisely said, 'Be still and know that I am God' (Psalm 46:10). Inner peace influences what and how we see externally. Michael Tubbs notes that:

> the good Samaritan came by, saw the man on the side of the road and looked and saw... a reflection of himself. He saw his neighbour, he saw his common humanity. He didn't just see it, he did something about it... He got down on one knee, he made sure the man was OK.[61]

---

61 Michael Tubbs, 'The political power of being a good neighbor' *TED Talk* https://www.ted.com/talks/michael_tubbs_the_political_power_of_being_a_good_neighbor

The greatest people are those who bend down in love. There are special people that walk through this earth with us, who have that golden touch, that gentle smile, that essential presence. The ordinary people who do simple things in beautiful ways. They are humane, they love and have a heart of flesh that is moved with compassion and urges them to action in the face of evil. Nothing more than solidarity is needed. One soul to affirm another.

Consider the consequences if we could stop and see and believe that each person has the possibility of being a 'Samaritan'. That the one before me is not my enemy and quite possibly better than I. If only we could see the good in others, as highlighted in Genesis 1:27, 'So God created humankind in his image, in the image of God he created them; male and female he created them'. Unfortunately, all too often Jesus refers to the failure of those around him, to see or understand.

> He said, 'To you it has been given to know the secrets of the kingdom of God; but to others I speak in parables, so that "looking they may not perceive, and listening they may not understand."' (Luke 8:10)

> 'Let these words sink into your ears: The Son of Man is going to be betrayed into human hands.' But they did not understand this saying; its meaning was concealed from them, so that

they could not perceive it. And they were afraid to ask him about this saying. (Luke 9:44-45)

Your eye is the lamp of your body. If your eye is healthy, your whole body is full of light; but if it is not healthy, your body is full of darkness. (Luke 11:34)

Then there are other examples of those who desire to see:

As he approached Jericho, a blind man was sitting by the roadside begging... Jesus stood still and ordered the man to be brought to him; and when he came near, he asked him, 'What do you want me to do for you?' He said, 'Lord, let me see again'. Jesus said to him, 'Receive your sight; your faith has saved you'. Immediately he regained his sight and followed him, glorifying God; and all the people, when they saw it, praised God. (Luke 18:35, 40-43)

He entered Jericho and was passing through it. A man was there named Zacchaeus; he was a chief tax-collector and was rich. He was trying to see who Jesus was, but on account of the crowd he could not, because he was short in stature. So he ran ahead and climbed a sycamore tree to see him, because he was going to pass that way. When Jesus came to the place, he looked up and said to him, 'Zacchaeus, hurry and come

down; for I must stay at your house today'.
(Luke 19:1-5)

So he set off and went to his father. But while he was still far off, his father saw him and was filled with compassion; he ran and put his arms around him and kissed him. (Luke 15:20)

The priest and Levite never got close enough to see who the victim was. They kept their distance. The message is that if we had the courage to look close at another, we just may well recognise our very own sisters and brothers there.

The Samaritan did come up close and personal to the man, so close that he was face to face. Maybe when he looked into that face he recognised one of his very own, and that is why he went to such extremes to assist. Or maybe he saw his very own self, reflected in the pain of the other.

Can we look into the face of another, into their eyes, and know the truth about them and ourselves? As the famous line from *Les Miserables* so aptly puts it, 'To love another person is to see the face of God'.

He was moved with pity...

The Samaritan 'was moved with pity' (v. 33). It is not just a fleeting moment of sadness. It is not a wistful memory. To be moved with pity is to have one's entire body respond and move into action. Meister Eckhart notes, 'Whatever God does, the first outburst is always compassion'.[62] We see this outburst of compassion throughout the Gospels.

> In those days when there was again a great crowd without anything to eat, he called his disciples and said to them, *'I have compassion for the crowd, because they have been with me now for three days and have nothing to eat. If I send them away hungry to their homes, they will faint on the way - and some of them have come from a great distance'.* (Mark 8:1-3)

> Jesus was left alone with the woman standing before him. Jesus straightened up and said to her, 'Woman, where are they? Has no one condemned you?' She said, 'No one, sir'. And Jesus said, *'Neither do I condemn you. Go your way, and from now on do not sin again'.* (John 8:7-11)

> One man was there who had been ill for thirty-eight years. When Jesus saw him lying there and knew that he had been there a long time, he said to him, *'Do you want to be made well?'* The sick man answered him, 'Sir, I have no one to put me into the pool when the water is stirred up; and while I am making my way, someone else steps

---

62 Matthew Fox, *Meister Eckhart: A Mystic-Warrior for Our Times*, (California: New World Library, 2014), 122.

down ahead of me'. Jesus said to him, 'Stand up, take your mat and walk'. (John 5:5-8)

Jesus, knowing that the Father had given all things into his hands, and that he had come from God and was going to God, got up from the table, took off his outer robe, and tied a towel around himself. Then he poured water into a basin and *began to wash the disciples' feet* and to wipe them with the towel that was tied around him. (John 13:3-5)

Luke's Gospel is unique in depicting God as touched to the inner core with pity. The Samaritan has a deep gut reaction to the injured man (10:33) and is moved to act because of the injustice he sees. This pity is also seen in the lost son's father (15:20), 'So he set off and went to his father. But while he was still far off, his father saw him and was filled with compassion; he ran and put his arms around him and kissed him'. It is also seen in the widow of Nain, 'When the Lord saw her, he had compassion for her' (Luke 7:13). Luke's Gospel also celebrates the God who chooses to be merciful not only to us, but to others, even those we would not otherwise have accepted into our fellowship.

The Samaritan had compassion, 'his heart was moved.' This is the only narrative parable in which the punch line occurs in the middle and not the end, explains Bernard Brandon Scott. When the man is attacked and left in the ditch half-dead, the audience recognises this as a hero story and awaits the arrival of the hero, with whom they will identify. They will ride to the rescue of the man in the ditch. Having begun the parable in expectation of playing the role of the hero, one ends in the role of the victim, being taken care of by one's mortal and moral enemy. The parable announces that the saviour is a Samaritan – the hated one.[63]

The Samaritan's act would certainly have been up for debate as Jesus told the parable to the crowd. What were the Samaritan's intentions? Why did he do it? We are suspicious of positive behavior by certain 'races' because we have become so cynical, assuming there are always ulterior motives. The parable challenges us:

Can we be present to others physically?

Can we be present to others emotionally?

What moves us to compassion?

What brings us to action?

What draws the best out of us?

How tenderly can we care for another?

What does it take to touch our hearts and seize our minds?

What is our attitude to the other?

Do our personal biases limit our ability to care?

---

[63] Bernard Brandon Scott, *Re-Imagine the World. An Introduction to the Parables of Jesus*, (California: Polebridge Press, 2010), 62.

Love will cost us. It will cost our identity. It is not to avert our gaze from what is ugly. It takes courage to buck the trend and show vulnerability. We risk ridicule or attack. But if we love courageously, and dare into the very sacred being of another, no one can stop us.

Who best to know the torments of others, but those who have experienced it too? Do we allow experience in our personal lives to make us a person for others, or do we deny our hurts and hide them out of sight? The Samaritan was moved with pity because he too had known suffering, what it means to be downtrodden. It becomes a blessing in disguise because we learn to empathise with others and to become more truly human. Otherwise, we become stuck in a false sense of superiority, like the priest and Levite, who are neither forced into humility, nor a deeper possibility of being more fully human. Have we too become:

- Hardened to the miseries of our world
- Sluggish to react
- Numb to respond
- Busy to care
- Important to notice others
- Cocooned to understand
- Self-centred to reach out
- Disgusted to look
- Emotionless to feel
- Intellectual to listen to the heart

Tired to care
Bitter to hope

What are our excuses? The Samaritan, despite a thousand excuses he could have made to justify walking on, chose instead to stop and to care.

Think carefully about what has made you get off the beaten track, to take risks, or to go out of your way. It was surely something that grasped at your heart. Without this impetus, we do not possess the inspiration to change the course we are currently on. So go back to the first question, 'What must I do to inherit eternal life' in verse 25. Your life will only be eternal when you can love each person, even the very least. When you open up your heart and listen to it, you will come to the insight that life is a journey of unexpected engagement and being. The Samaritan inherits eternal life because he understood the importance of love. He made every effort to give life to one who was dying. That is the crux, isn't it! To want eternal life you must be prepared to give and honour the life of others. To want eternal life, is to freely risk your life in the process.

The lawyer had it wrong, as did the priest and Levite. It is not about preserving your life. It is about using your life for the sake of granting life for others. Then eternal life is gained. As Jesus says:

> If any want to become my followers, let them deny themselves and take up their cross daily

and follow me. For those who want to save their life will lose it, and those who lose their life for my sake will save it. What does it profit them if they gain the whole world, but lose or forfeit themselves? (Luke 9:23-25)

Throughout Luke's Gospel, we see the image of a just and merciful God praised and applauded. This God of justice and love is what people seek. Below are a few such passages:

The Magnificat

For he has looked with favour on the lowliness of his servant. Surely, from now on all generations will call me blessed; for the Mighty One has done great things for me, and holy is his name. His mercy is for those who fear him from generation to generation. He has shown strength with his arm; he has scattered the proud in the thoughts of their hearts. He has brought down the powerful from their thrones, and lifted up the lowly; he has filled the hungry with good things, and sent the rich away empty. He has helped his servant Israel, in remembrance of his mercy. (Luke 1:48-54)

Jesus' mission

The Spirit of the Lord is upon me, because he has anointed me to bring good news to the poor. He has sent me to proclaim release to the captives and recovery of sight to the blind, to let the oppressed go free. (Luke 4:18)

I must proclaim the good news of the kingdom of God to the other cities also; for I was sent for this purpose. (Luke 4:43)

But I say to you that listen, Love your enemies, do good to those who hate you, bless those who curse you, pray for those who abuse you. If anyone strikes you on the cheek, offer the other also; and from anyone who takes away your coat do not withhold even your shirt. Give to everyone who begs from you; and if anyone takes away your goods, do not ask for them again. Do to others as you would have them do to you.

If you love those who love you, what credit is that to you? For even sinners love those who love them. If you do good to those who do good to you, what credit is that to you? For even sinners do the same. If you lend to those from whom you hope to receive, what credit is that to you? Even sinners lend to sinners, to receive as much again. But love your enemies, do good, and lend, expecting nothing in return. Your reward will be great, and you will be children of the Most High; for he is kind to the ungrateful and the wicked. (Luke 6:27-35)

> Do not judge, and you will not be judged; do not condemn, and you will not be condemned. Forgive, and you will be forgiven. (Luke 6:37)

In our deepest yearnings, our secret desires, our hidden dreams, we all possess one underlying element – love. To be love. To love. To be loved. The Samaritan is every person who has loved foolishly. As Micah succinctly puts it:

> He has told you, O mortal, what is good; and what does the Lord require of you but to do justice, and to love kindness, and to walk humbly with your God? (Micah 6:8)

Yet God loves even more than we do:

> The compassion of human beings is for their neighbours, but the compassion of the Lord is for every living thing. He rebukes and trains and teaches them, and turns them back, as a shepherd his flock. (Sirach 18:13)

The ultimate reason for our behaviour centres on our relationship with God. In coming to an awakening of Christ's presence, we come to a more healing, merciful and humble attitude towards ourselves and naturally towards others.

Chapter 7

Getting off the beaten track

He went to him and bandaged his wounds, having poured oil and wine on them.

Luke 10:34

He went to him...

The Samaritan must surely have been busy, but the beaten man took priority. Can we put aside our busy schedules to dare to be with another, with a stranger? All too often, people on the wayside of our path are ignored and dying, as we remain in our comfort zone, pretending to be oblivious to the wounds of the world. Yet God calls us to awaken to our responsibility for others.

In the parable of the rich man and Lazarus in Luke 16:19-31, the rich man neither sees nor approaches the poor man Lazarus, not unlike the priest and Levite.

> There was a rich man who was dressed in purple and fine linen and who feasted sumptuously every day. And at his gate lay a poor man named Lazarus, covered with sores, who longed to satisfy his hunger with what fell from the rich man's table; even the dogs would come and lick his sores. The poor man died and was carried away by the angels to be with Abraham. The rich man also died and was buried. In Hades, where he was being tormented, he looked up and saw Abraham far away with Lazarus by his side. He called out, 'Father Abraham, have mercy on me, and send Lazarus to dip the tip of his finger in water and cool my tongue; for I am in agony in these flames'. But Abraham said, 'Child, remember that during your lifetime you received your good things, and Lazarus in like manner evil things; but now he is comforted here, and you are in agony'. (Luke 16:19-25)

Lazarus experienced disgrace, hunger, shame, homelessness and abandonment. It was not his choice. He neither chose suffering freely nor wanted it, as he 'longed to satisfy his hunger' (Luke 16:21). Suffering is not something to be praised. In the parable, the one who suffers is given eternal joy, not because suffering earns them a place with God but because God wants to ease the person's anguish and give them the opportunity to flourish.

The rich man does not attain eternal life and it is not because he was rich. It was because he failed to do what God then had to do – ease the burden of the one who suffers. The rich man 'feasted sumptuously every day' (Luke 16:19). He chose to use his wealth to indulge himself. That is fine but when he has no regard for the other in need, the one at his very doorstep, that is when alarm bells sound! The rich man had the means and the capacity to aid another without any real cost or loss to his own self-entitlement, but the rich man failed to do so. The lesson is: no matter how small our act, it matters and is necessary, particularly service to the least.

No one is unworthy of our love and attention. The parable of the Good Samaritan actually narrows in on the least, the very ones we are unlikely to give our time for. It does so deliberately. The poor, the suffering, the lonely – their needs ought to be met. To ignore the least and simply accept that there is a gap between the rich and the poor – that life deals some people with fortune and others with bad luck – is an easy way out of our responsibilities.

People are hurting. People are ashamed. Healing hearts and healing hands are needed. It takes magnanimity, it takes courage, to stop and see and recognise and acknowledge the need right now of the powerless, the victimised, the grieving.

In preparation for the 2020/21 Australian Catholic Plenary Council, people were asked the question, 'What do you think God is asking of us in Australia at this time?' Being forgiving, generous and understanding, treating people with mercy, fairness and equality, and having greater sensitivity towards others were qualities suggested by participants. They provided numerous examples of the Good Samaritan and of supporting Pope Francis's vision of a Church of the poor and disadvantaged.[64]

Perhaps Martin Luther King Jr best sums up the Samaritan's correct attitude by the following words:[65]

> But I'm going to tell you what my imagination tells me. It's possible that those men were afraid. You see, the Jericho Road is a dangerous road... And you know, it's possible that the priest and the Levite looked over that man on the ground and wondered if the robbers were still around. (*Go ahead*) Or it's possible that they felt that the man on the ground was merely faking (*Yeah*), and he was acting like he had been robbed and hurt in order to seize them over there, lure them there for quick and easy seizure. (*Oh yeah*) And so the first question that the priest asked, the

---

64 Dantis, *Listen to what the Spirit is saying. Final Report for the Plenary Council. Phase 1: Listening and Dialogue,*' 38.

65 Martin Luther King Jr. *I've Been to the Mountaintop,* 3 April 1968.

https://kinginstitute.stanford.edu/king-papers/documents/ive-been-mountaintop-address-delivered-bishop-charles-mason-temple first question that the Levite asked was, 'If I stop to help this man, what will happen to me?' (*All right*)

But then the Good Samaritan came by, and he reversed the question: 'If I do not stop to help this man, what will happen to him?'

... and bandaged his wounds...

The parable makes clear how the Samaritan aids the injured man:

> He uses his own oil and wine
> Bandages the wounds
> Places him on his own animal
> Takes him to an inn
> Takes care of him
> Spends a sleepless night keeping watch
> Pays the innkeeper two denarii
> Promises to repay the innkeeper whatever more costs are incurred
> Promises to return

The Samaritan did what was within his means to assist the one in dire need. He offered first aid and more. To bandage the wound requires dealing with blood and pain, to assess and apply what needs to be done. It requires gentle touch and care. To comfort and be near and all the while possibly facing resistance or rejection by the victim.

The Samaritan makes a gift of his time and lends an outstretched hand. It is very much like Jesus who comes to the disciples behind closed doors. It is time for each of us to reach in and touch, as Jesus asked Thomas to touch the wounds. Richard Rohr notes that Jesus told Thomas:

> 'Put your finger here and see my hands. Reach out your hand and put it in my side' (John 20:27). Thomas was trying to resolve the situation mentally, as men usually do, so Jesus had to force direct physical contact with human pain – the pain of Jesus, Thomas' capacity for empathy with that pain, and very likely with Thomas' own denied pain. Deep healing has to happen corporeally and emotionally, and not just abstractly... This is the pattern of all authentic conversion in the Christian economy of grace: not around, not under, not over, but through the wound we are healed and saved.[66]

Offering genuine care becomes more than simply bandaging the wound. It becomes holistic care. It is journeying on another's road, at their pace, as their companion.

Of course today many would argue that 'bandaging a wound' is not enough. Social justice asks that we also

---

66 Richard Rohr, *On the Threshold of Transformation. Daily Meditations for Men*, (Chicago: Loyola Press, 2010), 256.

prevent the causes that lead to wounds. That is true, but the wound must also be tended too and the Samaritan does that and more. Dietrich Bonhoeffer listed:

> 'three possible ways in which the church can act towards the state'. The first was for the church to question the state regarding its actions and their legitimacy – to help the state be the state as God has ordained. The second way – was 'to aid the victims of state action'. He said that the church 'has an unconditional obligation to the victims of any ordering of society, even if they do not belong to the Christian community'. The third way the church can act toward the state, he said, 'is not just to bandage the victims under the wheel, but to put a spoke in the wheel itself'.[67]

In the parable, the Samaritan removed the victim from further harm and ensured the person's safety and possibility of recovery. He remains for the long haul. Perhaps also by his willingness to court danger on a treacherous and lonely road for the sake of assisting the wounded man, the Samaritan was making a public statement against the robbers. What he did was meant to be seen by all as in bold protest and opposition to those who chose to inflict harm against humanity.

---

67 Eric Metaxas, *Bonheoffer. Pastor, Martyr, Prophet, Spy. A Righteous gentile vs. the third reich*, (Nashville: Thomas Nelson, 2010), 153-154.

The Samaritan possessed extreme courage as well as extreme kindness.

Contrast the behaviour of the priest and Levite to the Samaritan or to Jesus who chose 'to wash the disciples' feet' (John 13:5) as an enduring act of love, one not to be forgotten so easily. The Samaritan and Jesus offer an act of service that forgets all troubles, removes all sense of shame, an act that recognises and reconciles. The Samaritan and Jesus risk betrayal, abandonment and ridicule. They invite us to such acts of kindness, 'So if I, your Lord and Teacher, have washed your feet, you also ought to wash one another's feet' (John 13:14).

Struggles, suffering and injustice will always plague our world but we are responsible for creating hope, community and goodness. Annie Dillard writes, 'Week after week, Christ washes the disciples' dirty feet, handles their very toes, and repeats, It is all right – believe it or not – to be people'.[68]

Acts of love and mercy are necessary for they are life giving. It is such qualities that enable people to do what must be done and it is such qualities that allow the recipient once again to live life.

Pope Francis is vocal about stepping out and doing good in the world rather than following a set pattern. He sees the church as a field hospital and

---

68 Annie Dillard, *Teaching a stone to talk. Expeditions and Encounters.* (London: Canongate, 2016).

not as a moralising powerful church that crushes the broken reed.

> The thing the church needs most today is the ability to heal wounds and to warm the hearts of the faithful; it needs nearness, proximity. I see the church as a field hospital after battle. It is useless to ask a seriously injured person if he has high cholesterol and about the level of his blood sugars! You have to heal his wounds. Then we can talk about everything else. Heal the wounds, heal the wounds... And you have to start from the ground up.[69]

A strong recommendation made by a number of participants for the 2020/21 Australian Plenary Council was for the Church to embrace a servant model of leadership that builds up community. This means humble service, authentic love of neighbour and visible leadership for social justice. There was a strong need felt to eradicate all attitudes of superiority, authoritarianism and entitlement.

> To embrace the weak and helpless, we have to become weak and helpless ourselves. We simply cannot serve from a position of power.

---

[69] Antonio Spadaro, 'A Big Heart Open to God: An interview with Pope Francis,' in *America. The Jesuit Review*, Sept. 19, 2013. https://www.americamagazine.org/faith/2013/09/30/big-heart-open-god-interview-pope-francis

A Church which 'acts justly, loves tenderly and walks humbly with God'. A community of faith, embedded in the Gospel, more communal and less hierarchical providing servant leadership which is respectful, encouraging and welcoming, meeting the needs of today realistically, being open to change, standing with and for the poor with courage and compassion.[70]

Along with building stronger communities, a large number of participants spoke about the need to welcome visitors, strangers, migrants, children, non-believers, the marginalised – homeless, lonely, divorcees and many others.[71] The parable of the Good Samaritan encapsulates the yearnings of the Australian people of God today.

... *having poured oil and wine on them...*

The Samaritan dresses the man's wounds with wine to disinfect and oil to soothe the pain. He uses everyday items as healing, soothing balm and antiseptic. Oil and wine were common in households, made by hand from natural resources people harvested from the land, including olives and grapes.

---

70 Dantis, *Listen to what the Spirit is saying. Final Report for the Plenary Council. Phase 1: Listening and Dialogue,*' 82-83.

71 Dantis, *Listen to what the Spirit is saying. Final Report for the Plenary Council. Phase 1: Listening and Dialogue,*' 161.

Today, there is a resurgence in natural methods and a growing interest in herbal medicines for healing, as opposed to medicinal treatments. Our grandparents, and even our parents, grew up in rural areas or villages that knew well the healing properties of plants, weeds, leaves, seeds and roots.

If someone is in need of healing, it involves, more often than not, our patient care, even if it is with the very little means that we have. It can be as simple as boiling aniseed and mint leaves to assist a person with stomach cramps. For a sore throat we gargle salty water or take a hot tea with lemon squeezed into it and add a large spoon of honey. It does not always take much to help ease the physical pain of the other.

The Samaritan only had oil and wine but he made the best use of it. We too in an emergency make best use of what we can where we happen to be. Yet how we provide these necessities is even more important. The Samaritan uses the oil and wine and then bandages the wound. How he applied them mattered even more. With gentle hands and encouraging words, the healing takes place.

The Samaritan then 'bandaged his wounds, having poured oil and wine on them' (v. 34). It was enough for the present moment, enough to allow physical healing to begin and enough to give impetus for the injured man to get away from the place of threat with the assistance of the Samaritan. To provide enough help to get the other out of the 'danger zone' and to a place or state of possible recovery, is all that is asked.

The Samaritan uses oil and wine to heal but these two elements also served other purposes. In the Old Testament, oil was seen as a sign of consecration and as a blessing.

> Then Moses took the anointing oil and anointed the tabernacle and all that was in it, and consecrated them. He sprinkled some of it on the altar seven times, and anointed the altar and all its utensils, and the basin and its base, to consecrate them. He poured some of the anointing oil on Aaron's head and anointed him, to consecrate him. (Leviticus 8:10-12)

> You prepare a table before me in the presence of my enemies; you anoint my head with oil; my cup overflows. (Psalm 23:5)

> Then I bathed you with water and washed off the blood from you, and anointed you with oil. (Ezekiel 16:9)

In the New Testament, oil is also used as a means of blessing:

> And a woman in the city, who was a sinner, having learned that he was eating in the

Pharisee's house, brought an alabaster jar of ointment. She stood behind him at his feet, weeping, and began to bathe his feet with her tears and to dry them with her hair. Then she continued kissing his feet and anointing them with the ointment. (Luke 7:37-38)

Are any among you sick? They should call for the elders of the church and have them pray over them, anointing them with oil in the name of the Lord. (James 5:14)

Wine is also an important symbol in the Bible:

And King Melchizedek of Salem brought out bread and wine; he was priest of God Most High. He blessed him and said, 'Blessed be Abram by God Most High, maker of heaven and earth; and blessed be God Most High, who has delivered your enemies into your hand!' (Genesis 14:18-20)

Wine to gladden the human heart, oil to make the face shine, and bread to strengthen the human heart. (Psalm 104:15)

The Samaritan had at hand oil and wine. He was prepared and ready to do what was needed. Maybe it is a lesson for the Church, for Christians, for all people, to always be prepared to offer freely our resources, to those in need. Our gifts are for the care of all and we have the necessary means for healing.

During the Offertory at Mass, the bread and the wine are taken up to the altar and become the Body and Blood of Christ, poured out for many as a life-saving action. The parable of the Good Samaritan compels us to question ourselves, what have we to pour out? What actions of ours are life-saving? What soothing balm do we carry, that can heal? What do we consecrate and what do we bless? The following, by an anonymous author, is food for thought:

> You are holding a cup of coffee when someone comes along and bumps into you, making you spill your coffee everywhere. Why did you spill the coffee? You spilled the coffee because there was coffee in your cup.
> Had there been tea in the cup, you would have spilled tea.
> Whatever is inside the cup, is what will spill out. Therefore, when life comes along and shakes you (which will happen), whatever is inside you will come out. It's easy to fake it, until you get rattled.
> So we have to ask ourselves... 'What's in my cup?'
> When life gets tough, what spills over?
> Joy, gratefulness, peace and humility?
> Or anger, bitterness, harsh words and reactions?
> You choose!

In the process of pouring out, we empty ourselves for another. Yet in our emptying we find ourselves being refilled with God's Spirit. Paul writes in Philippians 2:17, 'But even if I am being poured out as a libation over the sacrifice and the offering of your faith, I am glad and rejoice with all of you'. We also read in 2 Timothy 4:6, 'As for me, I am already being poured out as a libation, and the time of my departure has come'.

On the topic of healing, there are those who give their life to such a profession. Medical practitioners are required to take the Hippocratic Oath which states that:

> I will use treatment to help the sick according to my ability and judgment, but never with a view to injury and wrongdoing... Into whatsoever houses I enter, I will enter to help the sick, and I will abstain from all intentional wrongdoing and harm, especially from abusing the bodies of man or woman, bond or free.

The importance of aiding others is also mentioned in sacred texts of other religions:

> Serve Allah and ascribe no partner to him. Do good to your parents, to near of kin, to orphans, and to the needy, and to the neighbour who is of kin and to the neighbour who is a stranger, and to the companion by your side, and to the

wayfarer, and to those whom your right hands possess. Allah does not love the arrogant and the boastful. (Qur'an 4:36)

And he who saves a life shall be as if he had given life to all mankind. (Quran 5:32)

By serving each other you shall prosper and the sacrificial service shall fulfil all your desires. (Bhagavad Gita 3:10)

The parable of the Good Samaritan is a lesson in life that is embraced by other religions and cultures. In fact, Muslim Malaysian researchers AishathIffa Ashraf, NajyFaiz and Adlina Ariffin are calling for amendments to the Malaysian medical profession to include a codification of the moral duty to a legal duty, by enacting the Good Samaritan laws, where non-compliance will subject medical practitioners to some kind of retribution. In this way, it can be assured that society is being provided with the best standard of care, where no one is deprived of this basic need.[72]

---

[72] AishathIffa Ashraf, NajyFaiz and Adlina Ariffin, 'Imposition of Good Samaritan Laws to Improve Professionalism among Medical Practitioners' in *Intellectual Discourse*, Special Issue (2017) 673.

Chapter 8

Back on the road again

Then he put him on his own animal, brought him to an inn, and took care of him.

Luke 10:34

Then he put him on his own animal...

The Samaritan places the victim on his own animal. That takes great physical effort. It takes willingness and energy. How far are we prepared to go in assisting another? Or do we calculate the time, effort and cost, before we commit ourselves? Remember, we are not so much Christ bearers (*Theotokos*) as much as Christ bears us.

The Samaritan is like the shepherd who sought and found the lost sheep and placed him on his shoulders to bring him home:

> So he told them this parable: 'Which one of you, having a hundred sheep and losing one of them, does not leave the ninety-nine in the wilderness and go after the one that is lost

until he finds it? When he has found it, he lays it on his shoulders and rejoices. And when he comes home, he calls together his friends and neighbours, saying to them, "Rejoice with me, for I have found my sheep that was lost". (Luke 15:3-6)

It is the notion of carrying or assisting the one in need. The Samaritan does so. The shepherd does so. Simon the Cyrenean also does so. He carries the cross with Jesus because it cannot be done alone. We are all one in this together. We all have to face the tragedies of life, to carry one another's burdens and not to push the weak away when they need someone to lean on. Support is needed in difficult times and it should come from anyone. As Eugene H. Peterson writes, 'Original works of grace are possible in the everyday work of forgiving the sinner, in helping the hurting, and in taking up personal responsibilities'.[73]

There are levels of increasing humility that we can embrace on our roadside assistance. We see this through the gradual acts of the Samaritan. He begins with:

    Riding his high horse
    Comes down from his high horse
    Steps down into dirt
    Gets himself dirty

---

73 Eugene H. Peterson, *Traveling Light,* (Colorado: Helmers and Howard, 1988).

Carries the weight of another
Puts another on his own horse
Walks beside
Continues the journey

There is a time to get off our high horse and walk beside the other and with the other, arms around each other, on the journey, just as the Samaritan did. Jesus also accompanied the two who were on their way to Emmaus, 'While they were talking and discussing, Jesus himself came near and went with them' (Luke 24:15). Companion, friend, mentor or helper, who do we choose to be?

Who is our companion on the journey and are we companions to each other? One needs others there, to be with them, to stand by their side, to affirm beliefs that appear so frail, to be a support in vulnerability, to be on the lookout, keeping all harm away, someone there to hold, to love, to just be there in silence, a presence, a friend or a confidant.

Can we carry life's burdens and put our back to the plough? This is a vital question for all too often we renege on our responsibilities and leave others to pick up the mess we have left behind. The Samaritan did what the priest and Levite failed to do. He shouldered the burden and the pain of another. He chose to unite himself, identify with, participate in the struggles of another. He chose solidarity with someone very different and to do so is to enter a new world, a new way of understanding, to be open to new roads ahead and new possibilities, but along with it comes the risk of rejection.

The Samaritan uses his own animal to get the unidentified man back on track. It was lucky that the Samaritan had a means of transport to carry the man. Many at the time would have been walking the treacherous road on foot.

Carry this scenario forward to today, we take it for granted that we have transport to get us around. Bicycles, cars, trains, trams, buses, planes, taxis, ubers, etc. There are points to be taken from this. Number one: Many people walk miles as lack of infrastructure is a harsh reality in many countries. We ought not to take for granted the benefits we have. Number two: The pollution in our air is due in no small part to the many vehicles on the roads that spew out exhaust fumes. Do we consider how we travel and the best way to use the transport provided? Maybe our lockdown during Covid-19 made us more aware of our excessive use of our vehicles and the pollution it causes.

If we could take one lesson from the Samaritan that is pertinent to today, it is to use our own means of transportation, usually a car, to take others along with us. It would lead to a deeper encounter with the other, less congestion on our roads, a saving in fuel costs, and a better environment both naturally and with one another.

Today, it is not so much a choice but more so an imperative that we use our means of transport wisely. Eleven thousand scientist signatories from around the world, unequivocally declared that planet Earth is facing a climate emergency. What is required is that the world must quickly implement massive energy efficiency and conservation practices and replace fossil fuels with low-carbon renewables and other, cleaner sources of energy.[74] This argument is also supported by Pope Francis in his encyclical *Laudato Si'* (Praise be to you my Lord):

> Our difficulty in taking up this challenge seriously has much to do with an ethical and cultural decline which has accompanied the deterioration of the environment. Men and women of our postmodern world run the risk of rampant individualism, and many problems of society are connected with today's self-centred culture of instant gratification.[75]

Returning to the Samaritan, he places the beaten man on his animal in order to take him to a place of

---

[74] William J. Ripple, Christopher Wolf, Thomas M. Newsome, Phoebe Barnard, William R. Moomaw World Scientists' Warning of a Climate Emergency. *BioScience*, 05 November 2019.

[75] Pope Francis, 2015 *Laudato Si' (Praise be to you my Lord)*, paragraph 162.

http://m.vatican.va/content/francescomobile/en/encyclicals/documents/papa-francesco_20150524_enciclica-laudato-si.html safety and healing. The animal today can be considered our ambulance service, helicopters, or flying doctors, that transport the injured to a place of help. Yet these services are limited in their capacity due to restricted government funding. Yet, is not saving a human life worth tax-payers money?

The Gospels prioritise the needs of the fallen. Luke intended to show that in the parable of the Good Samaritan, becoming a neighbour, meant showing pity and kindness to those in need, even beyond the bounds of ethnic or religious groups. The Samaritan's mercy, risk, generosity and practical attention to the needs of the afflicted, indicate God's concern for those people whom others despise or condemned. God comes to bind up the wounds of the suffering, through unexpected love.

... brought him to an inn...

The Samaritan was not from the area so the choice was to leave the man where he found him, take him to an inn, or else take him home, which obviously was not close by. Now, of course, we could get hold of a doctor. Yet, back 2000 years ago, doctors and hospitals were not a common sight. So it was all up to the Samaritan.

The Samaritan chooses to take the beaten man to an inn. It would have been a tiring journey, considering there was a helpless person with him on a treacherous road. Yet, it mattered that the Samaritan took the man out of harm's way and put him up in a place where he could recover, no matter how far the distance. We are all but pilgrims on this earth or as Ram Dass puts it, 'we are just walking each other home'.

So they go to an inn. Inns and innkeepers had very dubious reputations at the time; yet in this case perhaps we can consider the inn an abbreviation for inner. The inner sanctum, where we hide from the outer world. The place where we meet with silence and quiet patient recovery.

The inn can also be considered akin to our hospitals, hospices, aged care facilities, or a Church threshold, where we can find rest and recuperate. The Church has for centuries founded hospices and hospitals, to care for those who need it. William Cavanaugh comments:

> The best kind of care that the church has provided for the world has been when it's out of power and it's not worried about ruling but more worried about being on the ground, taking care of the poor and the vulnerable.[76]

John Dickson further adds:

> During what's called 'Great Persecution' of years 303 to 312, many churches were destroyed and

---

76 The Good Samaritan - Centre for Public Christianity https://www.publicchristianity.org/the-good-samaritan/

Christians arrested and killed. Court records of the time highlight just how central charity was to the activities of the early church. Roman officials burst into the church of Cirta – over the other side of the Mediterranean – hoping there were treasures hidden in the basement, just as there often were in the pagan temples. What they found was a simple storage room for the church's work among the poor. The official records list the items: '16 tunics for men, 82 dresses for women, 13 pairs of men's shoes, 47 pairs of women's shoes, 19 peasant capes, and 10 vats of oil and wine for the poor'. Given Christianity's rich tradition of charity, I guess you could say they did find the true 'treasure of the church.'[77]

The Samaritan is a model of how the Church should be, what a Christian should be, or what a Jew should be, in fact, how each and every person should be, regardless of creed, gender and nationality.

... and took care of him...

Twice the word 'care' appears in the parable. In verse 34, we read, 'took care of him' and in verse 35 we have, 'take care of him'. We cannot deny that there are people in need, nor can we shirk from our responsibilities. As

---

[77] The Good Samaritan - Centre for Public Christianity
https://www.publicchristianity.org/the-good-samaritan/

Jesus said, 'For you always have the poor with you, and you can show kindness to them whenever you wish; but you will not always have me' (Mark 14:7). So what are we going to do about it?

We matter to one another and we need each other. We are better for knowing one another, and we can offer what the other cries out for – affirmation, support, dignity, meaning, loyalty and, most importantly, undying love.

The lesson for each person is to learn how to listen to the other, to hear their words of grief, to be attentive to their distress and agitation, and be moved by it. We need to put aside our needs, our tiredness, our fears, our angers, our prejudices, and be what the other needs of us, pleads from us, asks of us. We need to be disciples who truly care in times of suffering and can remain till the end.

If we carefully examine the parable, we can identify different types of care:

- The Samaritan started with presence and gentle care – the spiritual aspect.
- He moved to oil and wine and bandaging – the physical aspect.
- He stayed overnight and promised to return – the emotional aspect.

We all need constant care, ongoing attention, a healing presence. We need accompaniment and not to be left alone. We need healing, body, mind and spirit.

A Franciscan Benediction that calls us to be ready for the challenges that come each day reads as follows:

> May God bless you with a restless discomfort about easy answers, half-truths and superficial relationships, so that you may seek truth boldly and love deep within your heart.
> May God bless you with holy anger at injustice, oppression, and exploitation of people, so that you may tirelessly work for justice, freedom, and peace among all people.
> May God bless you with the gift of tears to shed with those who suffer from pain, rejection, starvation, or the loss of all that they cherish, so that you may reach out your hand to comfort them and transform their pain into joy.
> May God bless you with enough foolishness to believe that you really CAN make a difference in this world, so that you are able, with God's grace, to do what others claim cannot be done.

The message of the parable of the Good Samaritan is that we are meant to be social beings, in relationship with each other, caring for one another.

Chapter 9

The cost of being on the road

The next day he took out two denarii, gave them to the innkeeper, and said, 'Take care of him; and when I come back, I will repay you whatever more you spend'.

Luke 10:35

The next day...

So on the last leg of the journey, what can we expect to encounter? Well, then comes the next day, for nothing happens overnight. Nothing can be rushed in life, especially recovery from illness and grief. The road to recovery is a slow and long journey, where much needs to be re-built including:

    The value of trust
    Belief that people are generally good
    To walk alone without fear
    To recover from physical wounds
    To believe in one's self dignity and worth

The Samaritan does what he can to assist in the recovery, but he also knows how to pace himself. He organises himself to be present when needed, and to take a break, when necessary. Emeritus Pope Benedict's address in 2007, notes:

> Today we tend to defend our spaces of privacy and enjoyment too much, and we easily allow ourselves to be infected by individualistic consumerism. Hence, our option for the poor is in danger of remaining on a theoretical or merely emotional level, without truly impacting our behaviour and our decisions. What is needed is a permanent stance expressed in concrete options and deeds that avoids any paternalistic attitude. We are asked to devote time to the poor, provide them kind attention, listen to them with interest, stand by them in the most difficult moments, choosing to spend hours, weeks, or years of our life with them, and striving to transform their situation from within their midst. We cannot forget that that is what Jesus himself proposed with the way he acted and with his words: 'when you hold a banquet, invite the poor, the crippled, the lame, the blind.' (Luke 14:13)[78]

---

[78] Pope Benedict XV. General Conference of the Bishops of Latin America and The Caribbean *The Aparecida Document (TAD)* Aparecida, 13-31 May 2007, Paragraph 397.
http://www.aecrc.org/documents/Aparecida-Concluding%20Document.pdf

The Samaritan stayed and cared for the man overnight. The countless hours, the loss of sleep, the long nights, poised between life and death. The Samaritan kept vigil all night and yet Jesus' own disciples could not keep vigil in the Garden of Gethsemane (Luke 22:39-41, 45-46):

> He came out and went, as was his custom, to the Mount of Olives; and the disciples followed him. When he reached the place, he said to them, 'Pray that you may not come into the time of trial'. Then he withdrew from them about a stone's throw, knelt down, and prayed... When he got up from prayer, he came to the disciples and found them sleeping because of grief, and he said to them, 'Why are you sleeping? Get up and pray that you may not come into the time of trial'.

Good intentions may be there, and genuineness of heart may exist, but when it comes to putting faith into action, all too often we fail miserably. To love is a value we all hope to aspire to, but Jesus knew well our own weaknesses and selfishness, our betrayals and denials, our fears and failures.

Being there with the suffering for the long haul is a commitment we seem to be losing. In the past, the family had their elderly at home. They took care of them until their very last breath. In the past, mothers gave birth at home. The labour pains, the birthing and recovery all took place in the bedroom. In the past, the sick were looked after in their homes, resting while family members attended to their needs.

Today, we have handed over this responsibility of care to another. We do not grapple anymore with mess, with pain, with suffering. It is too difficult, too exhausting and too much of an inconvenience. We take them to an inn, no matter how dubious a reputation it has.

... he took out two denarii, gave them to the innkeeper...

The Samaritan offers to pay in order to ensure the wellbeing of the badly beaten stranger. The two denarii is the equivalent of two days wages for a labourer, so it is a significant amount. The Samaritan has given the man assurance and time to heal and recover.

He pays the innkeeper to look after the stranger, yet the Samaritan himself freely offered his services. Do we fall into the category of freely, willingly and generously offering care or has it become a profession, expecting payment in return?

Today there is ongoing debate about health care funding. Should it be privately funded or does the government have a responsibility towards making health care accessible to all? Yet this debate has not even been raised in many countries where the government contributes close to nothing in regards to health or education, child support or aged pension. So Jesus was well ahead of his time when he threw in the line:

> The next day he took out two denarii, gave them to the innkeeper, and said, 'Take care of him; and when I come back, I will repay you whatever more you spend'.

Care is necessary and ongoing, but it costs time and money and often the patient has little means to pay for a life-saving service. More so, it is through no fault of their own that they cannot access health care. So we either leave people to die in a rut, or we provide a means for their survival. The parable is clear: money is to be used to assist those in desperate need. Our choices are a matter of life or death and our money plays an important role in that.

How much money are we willing to part with, particularly for a stranger or for a cause not to our own benefit? In the past, Australians were very generous in their donations to charities but this has declined in recent years. Roy Morgan's Single Source survey – based on face-to-face interviews with more than 50,000 Australians during 2018 – found only 60 per cent of people donated to charity over a 12 month period, compared to 61.8 per cent in 2017 and 66 per cent in 2014.[79]

The attitude we have towards money matters. Just prior to the parable in Luke's Gospel, we have Jesus declare, 'Foxes have holes, and birds of the air have nests; but the Son of Man has nowhere to lay his head' (Luke 9:58), which is a worse predicament than our beaten man, who, through the generosity of the Samaritan, now has a place to lay his head, even if just for a night or two.

The use of our time and income matters. They matter most when donated to good causes, to the well-being of others, to creating a better world. Luke tells the parable of the rich fool, where the one who hoards his wealth and gains, will not live to enjoy it:

> Then he told them a parable: 'The land of a rich man produced abundantly. And he thought to himself, "What should I do, for I have no place to store my crops?" Then he said, "I will do this: I will pull down my barns and build larger ones, and there I will store all my grain and my goods. And I will say to my soul, Soul, you have ample goods laid up for many years; relax, eat, drink, be merry". But God said to him, "You fool! This very night your life is being demanded of

---

[79] Luke Michael, 'Experts Concerned as Fewer Australians Give to Charity,' in *Pro Bono News*, 25 February 2019. https://probonoaustralia.com.au/news/2019/02/experts-concerned-less-australians-give-charity/

you. And the things you have prepared, whose will they be?" So it is with those who store up treasures for themselves but are not rich towards God'. (Luke 12:16-21)

We have current evidence of what happens when we use our wealth for our own individual gains – materialism and consumerism, our unabashed ravenous greed that results in over production at cost and detriment to creation's balance and human livelihood. Pope Francis notes in *Laudato Sí*

> Today, however, we have to realise that a true ecological approach *always* becomes a social approach; it must integrate questions of justice in debates on the environment, so as to hear *both the cry of the earth and the cry of the poor.*[80]

Money is meant to ease burdens, ours and others, and not to cause grief and imbalance. Luke's Gospel insists that people use their money and possessions to care for the most vulnerably poor.

Sell your possessions, and give alms. (Luke 12:33)

---

80 Pope Francis, 2015 *Laudato Sí (Praise be to you my Lord)*, Paragraph 49.
http://m.vatican.va/content/francescomobile/en/encyclicals/documents/papa-francesco_20150524_enciclica-laudato-si.html

So therefore, none of you can become my disciple if you do not give up all your possessions. (Luke 14:33)

... *and said, 'Take care of him'...*

The Samaritan went out of his way and even above and beyond, to care for the unknown man. No one asked him to. It was his choice, his initiative, which arose from a compassionate heart able to empathise with the downtrodden. Yet at the inn, he makes a call. Turning to the innkeeper he clearly demands, 'Take care of him'. Ongoing care matters. What prompts one person to go out of their way to assist another may not necessarily be the case for all. In this instance, the innkeeper needed to be given instructions, a prodding, an incentive. Whether he followed through with it or not is another story to tell...

The innkeeper is to take care of the man. The Samaritan knows he cannot do it alone. Others must contribute to the healing process, people perhaps better qualified. Each person has something to offer. We all have a role to play, to take care of the other, for we are all caretakers.

When he saw the hungry crowd of thousands, Jesus tells the disciples, 'You give them something to eat' (Luke 9:13). Each one of us, no matter who we are, is called to be responsible for the other. There is no excuse. We all have some sort of capacity to care for the less fortunate, as the quote often attributed to Teresa of Avila, states:

> Christ has no body now but yours. No hands, no feet on earth but yours. Yours are the eyes with which he looks with compassion on this world. Yours are the feet with which he walks to do good. Yours are the hands with which he blesses all the world.

There is neither explanation as to why the innkeeper should take care of the stranger nor who the stranger is. It is simply the statement, 'Take care of him'. As we read throughout the parable, care ought to be an intrinsic part of our everyday activities and is not based on relationship, faith or nationality. Care is unbiased, freely given and without counting the cost.

'Take care of him.' But how? No direction is given, so what type of care are we meant to provide? Yet does it really matter? Care is just that and it is not prescriptive. It requires neither previous knowledge nor experience. Care is simply to attend to the needs of another as best we can. It is for a moment in time, where we have to turn our gaze away from ourselves and look upon another and see what they need. We have to reach out, and form a relationship with another in a way that is beneficial. This benefit may be physical or mental for the stranger, but it is also beneficial for ourselves, if not physically then at least spiritually. It is soul filling.

Today, with our mobile phones, ambulance at call, those trained in first aid, there is less of an excuse not to assist another. Yet people still avoid doing so. Perhaps it is not so much religious affiliation or nationality that prevents us from offering help today, but other diversions. So what holds us back from showing care?

> Do not know what to do
> Our time is taken up elsewhere
> Too many commitments
> Busy schedule
> Leave it with the experts
> I have done my part
> Not sure what else I can do
> They do not really need me

Yet do you think the beaten man wanted continued physical or financial help from the Samaritan? Probably not. So what do you think the beaten man wanted and waited for, from the Samaritan man?

> Company
> Opportunity to show gratitude
> A possibility to converse
> To become friends
> To journey together

New possibilities emerge when we can show compassion towards another, and in the process we shatter barriers and make mockery of stereotypes.

'Take care of him.' We are not given a choice. It is an imperative and prerogative. It becomes a necessity. To care cannot be limited by our excuses, by our picking and choosing who, where, when and what. God will come, whether we expect it or not:

> Listen! I am standing at the door, knocking; if you hear my voice and open the door, I will come in to you and eat with you, and you with me. (Revelation 3:20)

God will enter our abode unexpectedly and will want us to open our doors and hearts to whoever God brings along. If we allow God into our lives, to cross the threshold, then all whom God sends our way, must be welcomed.

... and when I come back...

There are times in life where we must part ways, even if for a brief moment. There are places we have to go to, roads we must travel on our own. But the paths taken should not be an avoidance or escape route. We cannot run away forever from what awaits us, although there is the belief that we can. We have to return eventually and 'put things right' otherwise we leave behind something incomplete that will surely linger with us as we try to journey on. There is no forgetting, no easy way out, no abandonment of our responsibilities. 'When I come back' is the possibility and promise of return. We need to be prepared, committed and to follow through.

Yes there are times we need to 'take a break' from our current circumstances in order to pursue other necessary callings, or just to rest and refuel, but what we have carried with us on our journey will remain with us wherever we go, either as a burden, or as a transformative effect, depending on our attitude to it. Jesus himself took time out to pray but always returned to minister. Below are some examples:

> At daybreak he departed and went into a deserted place. And the crowds were looking for him; and when they reached him, they wanted to prevent him from leaving them. But he said to them, 'I must proclaim the good news of the kingdom of God to the other cities also; for I was sent for this purpose.' So he continued proclaiming the message in the synagogues of Judea. (Luke 4:42-44)

> Now during those days he went out to the mountain to pray; and he spent the night in prayer to God. (Luke 6:12)

> Once when Jesus was praying alone, with only the disciples near him... (Luke 9:18)

> He was praying in a certain place, and after he had finished, one of his disciples said to him, 'Lord, teach us to pray, as John taught his disciples' (Luke 11:1)

We need to ensure we find time to rest and pray and refuel with the Spirit of God so that we can continue to offer ourselves to others in service.

... I will repay you whatever more you spend...

Together, we support each other and assist each other and that is why the Samaritan readily left the stranger in the hands of the innkeeper and promised to pay whatever else was necessary. The Samaritan did not have a monopoly on the beaten man.

We all have something to contribute to bettering society – our money, care, time, knowledge, experience and know-how. Every bit matters. We may be aware of better healing methods or medications that we can source out. The pursuit of health is important and each of us can offer ways to assist recovery.

The innkeeper needed enticement to care for another, which came in the form of monetary compensation, 'I will repay you whatever more you spend' (v. 35). Where has the ability to love unconditionally, to give freely, to offer genuine hospitality, gone? We incline our hearts to money in preference to the needy. If the Samaritan represents God's generous, ongoing offer of gracious love, then we, who are made in God's image, have strayed a great deal.

We, in our sensible attitude to life, with our many work demands, family expectations and personal needs, understand better than anyone else that we can neither save the world, nor assist every unfortunate person we encounter. It is impossible and in fact ridiculous to do so. The parable is far too extreme.

The Samaritan goes out of his way – that is acceptable – but he goes to the furthest degree. Okay, he stopped and assisted the beaten man, but also to stay with him overnight and then to pay all current and future expenses for a stranger – that is asking way too much of anyone. No one would expect that much from a stranger. A little help would be fine and would go a long way. In fact, that is all one would expect from a stranger.

So one may ask, is God the Samaritan in disguise? The God who comes to us as a stranger in our dire need, there beside us day and night, accompanying us as we recover? God the unexpected one, the generous one, the lover of all people, the one of boundless mercy, tender touch, generous love. But we can only be so much like God. We can give to others but surely not to this degree. It is impractical and impossible. It is costly and time consuming. It is unreasonable.

Does loving neighbour really mean to go all the way, to give ourselves up for the sake of the other? We can help, but only where we deem it possible in our very busy schedules and no one has the right to make unattainable demands on us. However, God does! As the quote by Zig Ziglar reminds us, 'There are 3 Cs in life: Choice, Chance, Change. You must make the choice, to take the chance, if you want anything in life to change.'

Chapter 10

The road ahead

> *Which of these three, do you think, was a neighbour to the man who fell into the hands of the robbers?' He said, 'The one who showed him mercy'. Jesus said to him, 'Go and do likewise'.*
>
> Luke 10:36-37

Which of these three, do you think, was a neighbour to the man who fell into the hands of the robbers?

The priest and the Levite kept their distance from the bleeding man. However, what one might justify by the law does not necessarily make it correct. In fact, approaching another, becoming a neighbour, was the only important law. The idea of the Israelites being the chosen people of God was not a tick of approval to be above others.

So Jesus has expanded the understanding of neighbour. It is not just a noun or a passive term. It is not the one next door to me. A neighbour is the one who approaches another in their time of need and lends a helping hand. The one who shows mercy. It has nothing to do with racial, religious or cultural backgrounds. It transcends these.

So the one who overstepped custom, ignored purity expectations, side stepped rituals, ignored racial backgrounds, overlooked religious differences, the radical, the one who dared, is the hero, the one to be praised.

If the commandment is to 'love your neighbour as yourself', then there are two criteria here we must consider:

- First, we must love ourselves in order to be able to love another.
- Secondly, if the neighbour is 'the one who showed' mercy (v. 37), then we must love the person in need, regardless of who they are.

So if the beaten man awakens and finds the Samaritan before him, he is called to acknowledge that the Samaritan behaved as his neighbour, and so he must love him, putting aside whatever hatred he may have previously held about Samaritans. The implications of this are significant. What comes to be the most important commandment is mercy and not the laws of the Torah that denounced Samaritans and other ethnic and religious groups. The ultimate claim on us is our acts of mercy.

We are meant to be neighbours, not strangers. We are meant to care, not to turn a blind eye. Jesus presents the Samaritan as a person to imitate. The ethnic and religious enemy is not only the story's hero but also the moral exemplar.

He said, 'The one who showed him mercy'.

Even the lawyer who wanted to test Jesus and probably dreaded the parable, still recognised the Samaritan as the one who was the neighbour and not the priest and Levite. The Golden Rule is, 'Do to others as you would have them do to you' (Matthew 7:12). Perhaps the lawyer realised if he was in the same situation as the beaten man, he would rather a law breaker be at his side than anyone else. We need mercy and healing, no matter who we are, and it should not matter from whom it comes.

The lawyer's response, 'The one who showed him mercy' (v. 37), is very telling. Mercy trumps everything else. Even the hardest of hearts cannot deny that mercy is the transformative factor. The lawyer, albeit reluctantly, admits that the Samaritan was the true neighbour because of his act of mercy, the one who behaved nobly.

Yet the lawyer's answer reveals his personal hardness of heart. He cannot bring himself to say the word 'Samaritan'. Instead he refers to the Samaritan as, 'he who showed mercy'.

Aesop's fables have been popular for over many generations but one of the most enduring of the fables is that of the sun and wind.

> The wind and the sun were disputing which was the stronger. Suddenly they saw a traveller coming down the road, and the sun said: "I see a way to decide our dispute. Whichever of us can cause that traveller to take off his cloak shall be regarded as the stronger. You begin". So the sun retired behind a cloud, and the wind began to blow as hard as it could upon the traveller. But the harder he blew, the more closely did the traveller wrap his cloak round him, till at last the wind had to give up in despair. Then the sun came out and shone in all his glory upon the traveller, who soon found it too hot to walk with his cloak on.

Kindness is more effective than severity! It takes gentleness, warmth and patience to draw out the best in another. The Samaritan did just that with the beaten man and so led him on the road to recovery. The lawyer recognised this virtue and acknowledge it, albeit reluctantly. 'Mercy, within mercy, within mercy' writes Thomas Merton.[81] That is what matters.

---

81 Thomas Merton, *The Sign of Jonas* (New York: Harcourt, Brace, 1953), 362.

Is this how we should behave towards one another then, mercifully? Not a popular word in today's society, as mercy gives a paternalistic vibe, as if we are superior to the other and out of our greatness we are stooping low to help someone far below our status. Would it be not better to offer something else – a free voucher, money, maybe a holiday, a loan, a massage, a beauty therapy session, indulgent pampering, or maybe a hamper with goodies? You can purchase some delightful products these days. We should focus on giving them a little gift to brighten their day, and we would have performed our good deed. But this mercy nonsense... No, we do not need to show mercy.

Or maybe it is perhaps more beneficial to be firm, get them back up on their feet, dust them off and send them on their way. They need to be self-sufficient and not dependent on handouts and generous benevolence. That only encourages laziness and dependence.

But slow down. Whether we like to admit it or not, there are people who need us desperately. They need our care, not our spare change! They need humanity by their side, not inanimate gifts.

We undervalue ourselves. We sell ourselves cheaply. What we have to offer others is much more than what we admit we can offer and there is more value in giving of ourselves rather than our presents. Presents and freebies and benefits might sound tempting to some but deep down what we all really crave for is true companionship, a gentle touch and deep love. Presence is more vital than presents.

We have to give of ourselves, not give of our possessions and wealth. They are a cover up to make us feel we have done something good. The parable is clear – give of yourself first and foremost. Who you are is what other people need, not what you have. Your empathy and compassion is not an act of sentimentality. Your love and mercy are not scorned by others. What will endure and create healing is our ability to see, hear and touch another in love. Giving anything else makes the other feel obligated towards you. Giving of yourself allows the other to open up in loving acceptance and response.

... Jesus said to him, 'Go and do likewise'.

Jesus concludes the dialogue by saying, 'Go and do likewise'. Jesus now asks the lawyer if he can apply the lesson to his own life.

Do we ever regret being virtuous? Unlikely. But there would be a long list of regrets when we fail to love. Yes, we may have been duped by people and others may have taken advantage of our better nature, but our reward is in knowing we did all we could. Over a century ago, when looking back on his life, Mark Twain wrote, 'There isn't time, so brief is life, for bickerings, apologies, heartburnings, callings to account. There is only time for loving, and but an instant, so to speak, for that'.

The parable and Jesus' pedagogical framing of it points to a particular relation between knowing and doing, thought and action. It is not enough to have solved the puzzle of the parable: to have identified the one who loves his neighbour. This is only the first step. 'Go and do likewise' means understanding and enacting the learning from the parable in the complexity of everyday life, writes P. N. Rule. As with the Samaritan, this might involve risks and costs. The parable opens out into the possibilities of an enactment of loving one's neighbour which cannot be prescribed but only lived.[82]

Jesus has moved the understanding and interpretation of the law by the lawyer from an exclusive, narrow minded view, to an all-inclusive practice. The lawyer should have left 'good enough' alone but now realised, when you want to face God, you must be prepared for life changing views. There is always more that we are called to, than our current limited ways.

> Jesus makes demands on us
> We cannot outsmart Jesus
> We cannot shirk our responsibilities

---

[82] Rule, P.N., 2017, 'The pedagogy of Jesus in the parable of the Good Samaritan: A diacognitive analysis', *HTS Teologiese Studies/Theological Studies* 73(3), p7. https://doi.org/10.4102/hts.v73i3.3886

> We know what is expected of us even though we feign ignorance
> In the end, our lives must reflect something of our understanding and belief of God

To be kind matters. To bear love is powerful. To show mercy is transforming. We are made for one another. We need each other. We are called to love. We love because we are made in God's image and 'God is love' (1 John 4:8). This is our calling.

In the Mass, we are also told at the end to 'Go!' We cannot sit back and allow the troubles of humankind to take care of themselves. We are part and parcel of life. Life is about going forth. A life of faith is a combination of action and contemplation and each informs the other. Prayer gives us the grace and impetus to be attentive to the needs of others, and our interaction and daily behaviours are the source of our prayers. Faith is about our presence in this world. This life is where our faith makes a difference. As James writes in 2:17, 'So faith by itself, if it has no works, is dead'.

Jesus desperately wanting his mission to continue, offered bread as nourishment saying, 'Do this in memory of me'. Do not forget. Keep my ministry going. And in his last final act, he performs his greatest service. Jesus gets down on his knees and washes the disciples' feet. How can they possibly forget now! Jesus offers parting words:

> I give you a new commandment, that you love one another. Just as I have loved you, you also should love one another. (John 13:34)

That is true discipleship, to love no matter the cost. Only such love can transform the world. Jesus' love is meant to endure all things. His love speaks the loudest. The longest. Do remember to serve and love. The Samaritan does precisely this.

In the end, love is all that matters and the parable has come full circle. What started off with a lawyer wanting to limit the commandments of the Torah, becomes in the end a life-giving, all-embracing commandment to love and to show mercy on the journey of life. There is no other way and there is no better way.

It is not about inheriting or earning eternal life. It is about living this life with love. So let us summarise the pattern of the journey outlined in this parable:

- At times, we are hesitant, questioning, stalling like the lawyer, wanting to 'test Jesus' and 'wanting to justify' ourselves. But if we do not take the next step, we remain in a rut. We do not need to have all the answers to life's questions before we commence our journey. The journey is so that we can answer life's questions.

The road ahead

- At times, we take paths that lead us to pain like the robbers and the beaten man, and we question why we took that road, made that decision. We question if life is worth living. We question the injustice and the suffering. Yet there is always the possibility of getting up and moving forward, if only we allow others to be by our side.

- At times, we walk through life so preoccupied with ourselves and our blinkered views that we do not notice what really matters, like the priest and Levite. We choose the easy road, what gives us security and ease, and at times we wonder if we are really travelling to anywhere important or just going around in circles, following the same routine. Maybe a jolt needs to happen to get our eyes off ourselves and back on the road, so that we can have a real destination and move forward.

- At times, we journey, fully embracing all that crosses our path. Open, accepting, loving and caring, we enjoy the challenge of inviting others with us, even if it means slowing down. Eventually we know that we will continue on, better for having accompanied another on the right track. And on goes the journey.

Such is life – hesitant starts, troubles along the way, self-protective periods, until we reach maturity of knowing our life journey is not just about me, but a journey of companionship and accompaniment.

So go and do what must be done. You are on the road of life. You are travelling. You will encounter others along the way. Do invite them along with you, or otherwise join their journey.

The road ahead

You were made by God, in God's image
to be like God for the world.
The Spirit of God is your very breath – allow it to
awaken you to new life.
Discipleship is your calling – use it to create
friendships and lasting relationships.
Pray that you may have eyes to see, ears to hear
and a heart of flesh.
Love your life and always choose life.
Be astounded, receive grace, give thanks.
Are you prepared to walk the narrow road,
making unpopular decisions,
with the interest of others at heart?
Be the love that is missing in the lives of many.
Challenge yourself, to forgive
time and time again.
Is it possible for you to sit with your enemies at
the same table and discover new alliances?
Can you appreciate the presence of those
around you?
Can you carry your cross while easing the
burdens of others?
Will you be moved to weep
at the wrongs of the world?
Remember that service to one another builds up.
Dry the tears of those who mourn.
Touch the wounds of those who suffer.
Comfort the distressed.

Soften those who have hardened their hearts.
Will you spend time alone in the desert places of
your soul?
Have you spent time being loved by the Creator?
Visit many people
as good company is always welcomed.
Fall into mercy, love unconditionally
give your all,
and in so doing you will live your life to the full.
Be Christ, for that is your calling
the best version of you. Amen.

Bibliography

Ashraf, AishathIffa; NajyFaiz and Adlina Ariffin. 'Imposition of Good Samaritan Laws to Improve Professionalism among Medical Practitioners.' In *Intellectual Discourse,* Special Issue (2017) 661–675.

Bausch, William J. *Storytelling: Imagination and Faith.* Mystic, CT: Twenty-Third Publications, 1984:117-137.

Bergstrom, Ted. 'The Good Samaritan and Traffic on the Road to Jericho.' In *American Economic Journal: Microeconomics* 2017, 9(2): 33–53 (pp49-50) https://pubs.aeaweb.org/doi/pdfplus/10.1257/mic.20150296

Benner, David G. *Human Being and Becoming. Living the Adventure of Life and Love.* Grand Rapids, Michigan: BrazosPress, 2016.

Bonyhady, Nick. 'Call for help': International response to Australian fires.' In *Sydney Morning Herald*, 6 January 2020.

https://www.smh.com.au/politics/federal/call-for-help-international-response-to-australian-fires-20200106-p53p5r.html

Bloem, Jeff. *An Economist Takes on the Parable of the Good Samaritan,* April 27, 2017. https://jeffbloem.wordpress.com/2017/04/27/an-economist-takes-on-the-parable-of-the-good-samaritan/

Brown, Neil. 'Uniting Faith and the Moral Life.' In *An Introduction to Catholic Theology,* edited by Richard Lennan. New Jersey: Paulist Press, 1998.

Dantis, Trudy; Paul Bowell, Stephen Reid and LethDudfield.*Listen to what the Spirit is saying. Final Report for the Plenary Council. Phase 1: Listening and Dialogue.* National Centre for Pastoral Research, Australian Catholic Bishops Conference, 2019. https://plenarycouncil.catholic.org.au/wp-content/uploads/2019/09/FINAL-BOOK-v7-online-version-LISTEN-TO-WHAT-THE-SPIRIT-IS-SAYING.pdf

Darley John M. and C. Daniel Batson. "From Jerusalem To Jericho": A Study Of Situational And Dispositional Variables In Helping Behavior. In *Journal of Personality and Social Psychology.* 1973, Vol. 27, No. J, 100.

https://greatergood.berkeley.edu/images/uploads/Darley-JersualemJericho.pdf

Dillard, Annie. *Teaching a stone to talk. Expeditions and Encounters*. London: Canongate, 2016.

Eliot, George. *The Mill on the Floss*. London: Penguin Classics, 1979.

Fox, Matthew. *Meister Eckhart: A Mystic-Warrior for Our Times*. California: New World Library, 2014.

Funk, Robert W. 'From Parable to Gospel: Domesticating the Tradition.' In *Funk on Parables: Collected Essays*. Santa Rosa, CA: Polebridge, 2006.

Ginott, Haim G. *Teacher and Child: A Book for Parents and Teachers*. London: Prentice Hall, 1993.

Gittins, Anthony J. *Called to be sent. Co-missioned as disciples today*. Oregon: Wipf and Stock, 2008.

Groome, Thomas H. *What makes us Catholic. Eight gifts for life*. NY: HarperSanFrancisco, 2002.

Guyon, Jeanne. *Experiencing the depths of Jesus Christ. One of the greatest Christian writings of all time. Library of Spiritual Classics*. Vol 2. US: SeedSowers, Christian Books Publishing House, 1975.

Hansberry, Lorraine. *A Raisin in the Sun.* Act III, Scene 1.
https://khdzamlit.weebly.com/uploads/1/1/2/6/1126-1956/a_raisin_in_the_sun_-_lorraine_hansberry.pdf
Judd, Naomi Judd. *Naomi's Breakthrough Guide.* Jan 6, 2004.

Julian of Norwich. *Revelations of Divine Love*
https://jesus.org.uk/wp-content/uploads/2015/05/revelations-of-divine-love.pdf

Kaylor, R. David. *Jesus the Prophet. His Vision of the Kingdom on Earth.* Louisville Kentucky: Westminster/John Knox Press, 1994.

King, Martin Luther, Jr. *I've Been to the Mountaintop,* 3 April 1968.
https://kinginstitute.stanford.edu/king-papers/documents/ive-been-mountaintop-address-delivered-bishop-charles-mason-temple

Levine, Amy-Jill, *Go and Do Likewise: Lessons from the parable of the Good Samaritan,* 17 September 2014https://www.americamagazine.org/faith/2014/09/17/go-and-do-likewise-lessons-parable-good-samaritan

Martin, James. *Jesus. A Pilgrimage.* New York: HarperOne, 2014.

Merton, Thomas. *Conjectures of a Guilty Bystander.* New York: Bantam Doubleday Dell Publishing, 1994.

Merton, Thomas. *The Sign of Jonas.* New York: Harcourt, Brace, 1953.

Metaxas, Eric. *Bonheoffer. Pastor, Martyr, Prophet, Spy. A Righteous gentile vs. the third reich.* Nashville: Thomas Nelson, 2010.

Michael, Luke. The acts of kindness shining through as coronavirus panic takes hold, 20 March 2020. https://probonoaustralia.com.au/news/2020/03/the-acts-of-kindness-shining-through-as-coronavirus-panic-takes-hold/

Nyquist, J. Paul *Is Justice Possible? The elusive pursuit of what is right.* Chicago: Moody Publishers, 2017.

Peterson, Eugene H. *The Contemplative Pastor. Returning to the Art of Spiritual Direction.* Grand Rapids, Michigan: William B. Eerdmans Publishing Company, 1989.

Peterson, Eugene H. *Traveling Light*. Colorado: Helmers and Howard, 1988.

Pope Benedict XVI, V General Conference of the Bishops of Latin America and The Caribbean *The Aparecida Document (TAD)* Aparecida, 13-31 May 2007. *http://www.aecrc.org/documents/Aparecida-Concluding%20Document.pdf*

Pope Francis, *Laudato Sí (Praise be to you my Lord),* 2015, paragraph 162. http://m.vatican.va/content/francescomobile/en/encyclicals/documents/papa-francesco_20150524_enciclica-laudato-si.html

Pope Francis, *Aperuit Illis*, Instituting the Sunday of the Word of God, 30 September 2019. http://www.vatican.va/content/francesco/en/motu_proprio/documents/papa-francesco-motu-proprio-20190930_aperuit-illis.html

Rindge, Matthew S. *Good Samaritan (Luke 10:25-37),* n.p. [cited 5 Jun 2019]. https://www.bibleodyssey.org:443/en/passages/main-articles/good-samaritan

Ripple, William J, Christopher Wolf, Thomas M Newsome, Phoebe Barnard, William R Moomaw.

'World Scientists' Warning of a Climate Emergency.' In *BioScience*, 5 November 2019.

Rohr, Richard. *On the Threshold of Transformation. Daily Meditations for Men.* Chicago: Loyola Press, 2010.
Romero, Oscar. *Daily Meditations.* 26 November 1978;Translated by Irene Hodgson. St Anthony Press, 2005.

Rule, P. N. The pedagogy of Jesus in the parable of the Good Samaritan: A diacognitive analysis.' In *HTS Teologiese Studies/Theological Studies* 73(3), 2017.

Samaritan's Purse. International relief Australia and New Zealand.
https://www.samaritanspurse.org.au/who-we-are/about-samaritans-purse/

Scott, Bernard Brandon. *Re-Imagine the World. An Introduction to the Parables of Jesus.* California: Polebridge Press, 2010.

Sheldrake, Philip. *Spirituality and Theology: Christian Living and the Doctrine of God.* Maryknoll, NY: Orbis Books, 1998.

Slick, Matt. *The Good Samaritan Luke 10:25-37*https://carm.org/parable-good-samaritan

Spadaro, Antonio. 'A Big Heart Open to God: An interview with Pope Francis'. In *America. The Jesuit Review*, Sept. 19, 2013. https://www.americamagazine.org/faith/2013/09/30/big-heart-open-god-interview-pope-francis

Survivor Australia: GoFundMe for Luke surpasses Pia's prize money https://www.news.com.au/entertainment/tv/reality-tv/australian-survivor/survivors-luke-toki-on-track-to-surpass-winning-prize-with-viral-gofundme/news-story/af119d0df2ac6175837e45f95f78aa11

The Universal Declaration of Human Rights. United Nations 2015. https://www.un.org/en/udhrbook/pdf/udhr_booklet_en_web.pdf

Tolle, Eckhart. *The Power of Now. A guide to spiritual enlightenment.* California: New World Library, 2004.

Tolstoy, Leo. *War and Peace,* Trans. Louise and Aylmer Maude. Oxford: Oxford University Press, 2010.

Tubbs, Michael. 'The political power of being a good neighbour.' In t*endD Ideas worth spreading,* April 2019. https://www.ted.com/talks/michael_tubbs_the_political_power_of_being_a_good_neighbor

Tverberg, Lois. *Jesus' Surprising Answer* June 5, 2019 https://engediresourcecenter.com/2019/06/05/jesus-surprising-answer/

Varengo, Peter. *We want to see Jesus. Discipleship as a journey of search and commitment.* Victoria: Coventry Press, 2018.
What is the meaning of the Parable of the Good Samaritan?' in *Got Questions. Your Questions. Biblical Answers.* https://www.gotquestions.org/parable-Good-Samaritan.html

www.ingramcontent.com/pod-product-compliance
Lightning Source LLC
Chambersburg PA
CBHW010245010526
44107CB00063B/2689